"*Clickety Clack* is the story of an accomplished woman for whom life has not been easy. Her victory over her illnesses, mental and physical, makes for inspiring, informative reading. Wisdom comes from the shared experience."

MARY V. SEEMAN, O.C., M.D., Professor Emerita, Department of Psychiatry, Centre for Addiction and Mental Health, University of Toronto, Canada, pioneer in women's mental health issues and well known for her work on schizophrenia in women.

"There's incredible material in *Clickety Clack*…This telling of the 'ride' has perpetually disturbing undercurrents that evidence what every reader has to grudgingly admit: the very real and literal fear of mental illness. Through its chilling detail, the reader gets the sense of 'self-purging from purgatory' and the personal search for some sense of what has happened to succour life."

CYNTHIA P. HUBLER, Manchester, Connecticut, patient advocate and mother of a bipolar disorder daughter

"I couldn't take *Clickety Clack* all in on the first read, so I read it again, this time with my seat belt fastened. It is a courageous act to take on a project and to write it all, especially to revisit and face up again to those fearfully painful times. I have learned about the author's evolved character and her life's trajectory and I understand, too, how she could not not write this book."

CYNTHIA A.M. POWELL, Fairfield, Connecticut, childhood friend of Joy S. McDiarmid

"*Clickety Clack* has the virtue of making the reader see and feel what it is like to be mentally ill. So many people are born into suffering and terrible circumstances that are beyond their control. Joy's life reminds us of that fact. Her story presents, in some sense, as human suffering itself. Although the book is tough going at times due to the intensity of the writing, Joy's story is, in the end, inspirational. She always finds a way.

MICHAEL I. ALEXANDER, author of *How to Inherit Money* and *Competing Against America*

"This book is way more than I expected it to be. I honestly expected to read a personal recounting that would prove little more than a vehicle for the author's cathartic venting, but Joy McDiarmid blew me away both with the quality of writing and the story itself. It's a huge bonus that she enlisted the participation of a co-author with bona fide medical and academic credit. Having Dr. Edye summarize each chapter and offer additional information and insight is brilliant and really changes the dynamic of the book in terms of its ability to reach a broad audience."

MEG McALLISTER, communications specialist, Toronto and New York

Clickety Clack

My Bipolar Express

Joy S. McDiarmid

Joy S. McDiarmid

Medical commentary by

Frances W. Edye, M.D.

Blue Butterfly Books

THINK FREE, BE FREE

Blue Butterfly Book Publishing Inc.
2583 Lakeshore Boulevard West, Toronto, Ontario, Canada M8V 1G3
Tel 416-255-3930 Fax 416-252-8291 www.bluebutterflybooks.ca

Complete ordering information for Blue Butterfly titles is available at:
www.bluebutterflybooks.ca

First edition, soft cover: 2010

LIBRARY AND ARCHIVES CANADA CATALOGUING IN PUBLICATION

McDiarmid, Joy S. (Joy Suzanne), 1939–
Clickety clack : my bipolar express / Joy S. McDiarmid ; medical commentary by Frances W. Edye.

Includes index.
ISBN 978-1-926577-02-9

1. McDiarmid, Joy S. (Joy Suzanne), 1939– —Mental health.
2. Manic-depressive persons—Canada—Biography. I. Title.

RC516.M29 2009 362.196'8950092 C2009-904227-4

Design and typesetting by Gary Long / Fox Meadow Creations
Front cover concept and photo by Joy S. McDiarmid
Text set in Adobe Garamond and Optima
Printed in Canada by Transcontinental-Métrolitho
Text paper contains 100 per cent post-consumer recycled fibre

Blue Butterfly Books thanks book buyers for their support in the marketplace.

This book is dedicated to
those who live what I voice here

You gain strength, courage and confidence by every experience in which you really stop to look fear in the face. You must do the thing you cannot do.

Eleanor Roosevelt

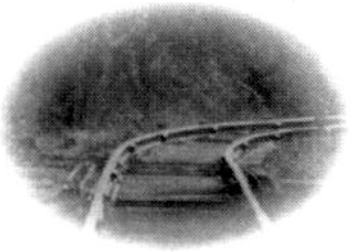

Author's Note

The events and persons in this book are real. However, to protect the privacy of certain individuals, in some cases pseudonyms are used and personal descriptions altered.

Photographs are courtesy of the author, except for the newspaper clipping from the *Winnipeg Free Press*. Sections of this book might well have been accompanied by photographs, as a number of the early chapters are, but the author destroyed most of them for their too-painful memories.

Part of the proceeds from the sale of this book will go to The Joyful Fund, established by Joy S. McDiarmid in 2000. Administered by The Winnipeg Foundation, it is named in honour of Joy's many friends who gave her the moniker Joyful. Earnings from the fund are used specifically for women who struggle with bipolar disorder or schizophrenia and who, in recovery, wish to further their education to hasten re-entry into the workplace.

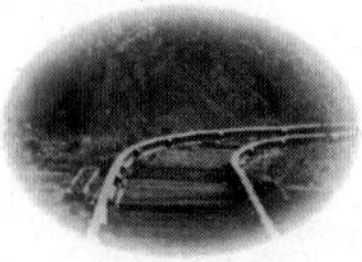

Contents

Foreword by Dr. Frances W. Edye *xv*

Beginnings *xviii*

CHAPTER 1 Birth Day *1*

CHAPTER 2 Shadows on the Walls *13*

CHAPTER 3 Haunting *19*

CHAPTER 4 The Queen is Coming… *37*

CHAPTER 5 Gender Identity *46*

CHAPTER 6 Sexual Identity *55*

CHAPTER 7 Electroconvulsive Therapy *64*

CHAPTER 8 Empty Mirror *80*

CHAPTER 9 Heydays *91*

CHAPTER 10 Living on the Edge *101*

CHAPTER 11 Memoirs of Madness *118*

CHAPTER 12 Demons in the Dungeon *128*

CHAPTER 13 Dear Josephine *142*

CHAPTER 14 Hospital Nightmares *148*

CHAPTER 15 It's a Family Thing *161*

CHAPTER 16 The Roundhouse *170*

Epilogue 178

Index 180

Credits 183

Interview with the Author 187

Foreword

by Frances W. Edye, M.D.

I am a psychiatrist's in private practice in Winnipeg, where I also do consultation work with various organizations. For the past fifteen years, I have worked extensively with communities in the near and far north, and also provided telepsychiatry for First Nations and Inuit communities. I am a lecturer at the University of Toronto and assistant professor at the University of Manitoba.

Clickety Clack is a very human, engaging, and truthful story about Joy McDiarmid's experiences with bipolar disorder, as well as with other psychiatric and physical challenges, which she has faced every day of her life. I recommend this book in the full knowledge that you will learn much from Joy's struggle and her account of society's harsh judgments concerning mental health issues.

While *Clickety Clack* is not a clinical book, Joy makes reference to some clinical terms. So that you can better understand Joy's very human story, I have explained these in my commentary at the end of the chapters.

Bipolar disorder is an unkind, pervasive, profound mental illness that knows no end. It creates chaos, wreaks havoc, steals lives, invades the family dynamic, and is unrelenting in its grip. In any given year, it presents a human tragedy for some two million North Americans. In a recent study of people suffering from the condition, thirty-one percent reported that their disorder appeared before the age of eighteen, although in some cases, it has emerged in children as young as ten. Studies also suggest that bipolar disorder begins in childhood, as it did for Joy, usually in the form of disruptive behaviour or mood changes.

The condition has many other presentations. It cycles between a manic, expansive personality, characterized by lavish spending and outlandish, elevated behaviour that can become psychotic, and depressive states characterized by a negative outlook on life, deep mood fluctuations, insomnia, feelings of worthlessness, and suicidal and self-destructive thoughts, all of which bring anger, nightmares, restlessness, marital discord, and an inability to adhere to social norms.

It is quite common for a person who struggles with bipolar disorder to meet the full diagnostic criteria of other illnesses, such as panic disorder, obsessive compulsive disorder, and social phobia. Another common co-diagnosis is substance abuse, often with alcohol, cannabis, or cocaine.

Bipolar disorder with psychosis can sometimes be difficult to distinguish from schizophrenia, particularly at an early stage in the illness. Schizophrenia, a debilitating illness that often strikes for the first time when people are in their early twenties, includes symptoms such as distortions of reality, auditory or visual hallucinations, and an overall deterioration in function.

In schizoaffective disorder, which is part of the spectrum of schizophrenic disorders, a person who meets the full diagnostic criteria for a mood disorder such as bipolar disorder can also meet diagnostic criteria for schizophrenia. Furthermore, a person with schizoaffective disorder can also have delusions or hallucinations even when mood symptoms are not present.

Treatment for some who suffer from bipolar disorder and schizoaffective disorder has been expanding. A wide range of mood stabilizers, antidepressants, and anti-psychotic medications are now available. Some of these need to be taken for a lifetime. Each, however, can have mild to severe side effects, which include increased risk of obesity, diabetes, high cholesterol, and coronary artery disease. Some of these side effects are compounded by lifestyle factors that often affect people with mental illness, such as lack of exercise and sedentary daily routines. To manage these problems effectively, a patient's treating psychiatrist and family doctor should work together in a holistic way.

Joy and I have worked together since 2002, after her previous psychiatrist retired. Though Joy has clearly met diagnostic criteria for bipolar disorder, she has had a number of other difficulties and struggles. Joy also experiences sexual and gender issues, which will be addressed in later chapters.

My role in this book is to add a medical commentary to Joy's story to promote a greater understanding of the major aspects of Joy's life-long disorders and her struggle to live her life to its highest potential.

Frances W. Edye

Winnipeg
May 25, 2009

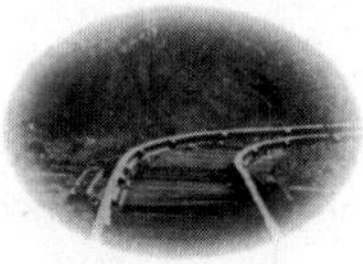

Beginnings

This is a true story. Nature, nurture, and heredity had a collision. A big bang. My birth was a cold, unwanted, unplanned, and empty event. While I was growing up, there were oddities, infirmities and "secrets," but I couldn't tell anyone about them. Now I must.

This book is about my life and how it has been affected by bipolar disorder, also referred to as manic depression. This disorder carries symptoms such as depression, mania, anxiety, social phobia, obsessive-compulsive behaviour, psychosis, sexual and gender issues, magical thinking and its behavioural aspects, and recurring difficulties associated with relationships, work, and hospitalization.

Writing of all of this, bringing it out in the open, has been a difficult but cathartic process. Much of my life unfolded in times when family secrets like alcoholism, divorce, suicide, and mental illness were confined to a dark closet. That door remained closed tightly. It was a betrayal to hint at any truth. It was the way of my world.

My life has held both kindness and terror. I was an only child, who was ignored and left to exist in a very active imaginary life. This set the stage for bipolar disorder. My condition occurred with psychosis, or more properly, schizophrenia spectrum, a profound and frightful form of bipolar disorder that lasts a lifetime. Bipolar disorder was prevalent in my mother's family and also in my father's. It is known to manifest itself with more intensity in each generation. The high heritability rate, coupled with my psychosocial stressors, meant that I got the candy box prize!

My purpose in writing *Clickety Clack* is to provide helpful information for anyone on a similar journey. With that end in mind, I've written the book in the first person in the hope of engaging the reader in an intimate conversation.

The content of this book is enhanced by the commentary by Dr. Frances Edye, a noted Canadian psychiatrist who specializes in the field of bipolar disorder. At the end of each chapter of my story, she provides commentary that promotes understanding of major aspects of this disorder.

......

Now it's time to tell you about Clickety Clack. The title of this book is taken from the noise train wheels make when hitting the joints in railway tracks. The cover photograph shows a beautiful but daunting mountain traverse; the track veers distinctly to the right, as did my life.

The train, created in my imagination when I was a child, hurtles through the night. Its destination is known; mine is not. My imaginary train has a wonderful red caboose, the kind you want to wave to when it goes by. The caboose has always been my refuge, and it has taken me on part of the journey portrayed in this book.

Inside, the caboose has living space for three men. It's about ten feet wide and forty feet long. The walls are dark wood and the floors are sometimes painted bright red. There are three beds on the main floor, one for the conductor (beside his desk), one for the brakeman, and one for me when I visit during the night. Also, there are closets, storage cupboards, folding tables, dishes, an icebox, a water tank, a sink, and, of course, a wood stove. No potty, however. (Hearty young men go outside for that.) Upstairs, beside each seat, two long windows provide a sweeping view of the world as it passes by. When the men aren't working, the seats are a cozy place for conversation.

I have many fond memories of my visits to the caboose, but only bad memories of the baggage car attached to it. There I dumped my terrible thoughts, rough experiences, and troubled dreams before I slipped into the caboose.

My imaginary playmates inside the caboose were my saviours: Mr. McTavish, the conductor, and Ernie, the rear brakeman. They were my source of comfort, understanding, and equilibrium. The caboose was a place to go to tell tales of woe, to be soothed, to voice harms, indiscretions, and the misdirection of adult words. With the help of Mr. McTavish and Ernie, I stayed on track, no matter how many twists and turns the train took through the mountain passes. Every night after my prayers, I could close my eyes and see the faces of my two friends. Then I was safe. I still go to the caboose from time to time. It lives on as a place where I can make soft landings.

……

I've searched relentlessly most of my life to better understand bipolar disorder and its many manifestations. To manage the disorder, I've had to read endlessly, talk to mental health professionals on a regular basis, and spend time with other sufferers in support groups.

I hope that you will find in *Clickety Clack* an interesting and informative story; it is a portrait of my journey to learn how to live a hidden life in the open. I also hope that you will gain a greater understanding of the challenges that sufferers face everyday. Perhaps, in the end, you will be the person who leads an army to diminish the stigma that plagues us.

Two people who read drafts said, "Now, do you feel better?" I was miffed in both cases, but now realize that I should have responded, "I am proud that I was able to slay dragons to get the words on pages of this manuscript. And, I am more confident, now, of my ability to continue my life, since I know that I have contributed ideas that may help others to slay some of their demons."

In "Do Lord Remember Me"* The Reverend Joshua Smith Sr. describes the course I needed to travel to write this book: "...[O]nly now, when there was nothing but past, did it surface to be explained and lived truly for the first time." That is where the true lessons of words begin—in honesty and intimacy.

Joy S. McDiarmid

Victoria Beach, Manitoba
June 1, 2009

*In Margaret Fowler and Priscilla McCutcheon, eds., *Songs of Experience: An Anthology of Literature on Growing Old* (New York: Ballantine Books, 1991).

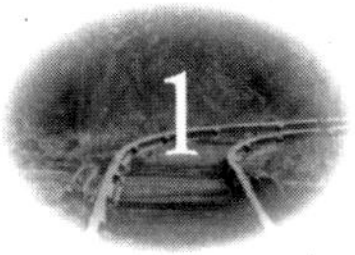

1 Birth Day

When I was a child, I was hungry for stories. Like most children, I wanted to know details of people and events that affected my little life. None were told in my house, however. My parents excluded me from most of their life together, and certainly never included me in their discussions or stories, at bedtime or otherwise. Luckily, I did hear many stories from my beloved maternal grandmother, Lou Little. Everyone in the family called her Dee. Apparently I gave her that name; after hearing her referred to so often as "dear Lou," and being unable to say "dear," I coined the name "Dee," which became an endearment for the rest of her life. Dee loved to tell stories, and so I was never disappointed. And yet, that wasn't enough. I wanted more from my parents, particularly my mother.

I saw little of my parents during the first five years of my life. During that time, I lived with Dee on and off at her home at 890 Palmerston Avenue in Winnipeg. Initially, I was entrusted to Dee's care as a result of my mother's illness following my birth. Then, during the following few years, my parents travelled extensively, so I spent most of my early life living with Dee. I dearly loved my grandmother, but I yearned for my mother, and although I didn't cry when my parents were away, I felt alone and lonely. As a family, we finally came together in a small River Heights house late in my fifth year, soon thereafter moving into a duplex on Grosvenor in time for me to start kindergarten.

My grandmother's large home was on the Red River in the west end of Winnipeg. I'm told this old grey house was a hubbub of activity during the Second World War years. On some weekends, it was filled with parties given by Dee or her children—her son, Wib, her older daughter, Glad (my mother), or younger daughter, June. On occasion, the house brimmed with air force servicemen, who enjoyed the rousing entertainment of piano music and singing.

Dee would often tell me stories about my early childhood. Sometimes I would sit on her knees, or she'd prop me up in her bed under a cozy satin duvet, or we'd sit in front of a fire in the stone fireplace that was the centrepiece of the family log cottage at Victoria Beach on Lake Winnipeg. When I was a little older, I would linger over a cup of tea, as another story unfolded in Dee's yellow kitchen on Girton Boulevard in Tuxedo, a village in the south end of the city to which she moved after the great flood of 1950. Among the many stories Dee told me, my favourite was the one about the events surrounding my birth on December 7, 1939.

It's important that you know Dee's stories were told to give me a sense of my early childhood, a background that she knew I would not find elsewhere. She was a master storyteller who could paint a picture with words alone. And she understood that she needed to wait until I was an appropriate age before telling me about my earliest days. She also had infinite patience. Over and over again I would have her tell me some of the same stories so that they would become imprinted on my mind. Dee gave me words to hold on to that made me brave, salved my loneliness, and taught me important lessons.

This is the story I heard of my impending birth. It's a combination of what Dee said and my impressions taken from her words or plumbed from a few stark facts perched in my mind.

On the afternoon of December 6, 1939, Dee told me that she was dressed, as she often was, in a dark blue skirt matched by twin cashmere sweaters and a pair of dark blue shoes. Her jewellery was always fine, complementing her blonde collar-length hair and stately appearance. This day was no exception. She wore a simple single strand of pearls, a pair of button pearl earrings, and an opal and pearl ring.

Dee sat in the sunroom, which overlooked the then-frozen Red River. The sunroom was decorated in chairs and chaises in various shades of beige, each with a bold pattern of sweeping blue willows. The room welcomed visitors into the warmth of person and place. As was her custom every weekend, she sat at the writing desk in the room, penning a letter to her sister in Duluth. Her other weekend enjoyment had been a ride on her horse, Danny Boy, a magnificent steed with a shiny black coat.

That afternoon, Glad, my mother, walked from the Capital Theatre in downtown Winnipeg to 890 Palmerston—a healthy hike, but she was just twenty-four. She had seen a glorious new film, *Gone with the Wind*, starring Vivien Leigh and Clark Gable, he of the famous line, "Frankly my dear, I don't give a damn!" The sweeping film had caught Glad's imagination, and she was eager to share her impressions with her mother. Lou waited patiently for Glad but worried because she had only about three weeks to go in her pregnancy.

A mere ninety-eight pounds on her wedding day three years before, Glad held the eyes of everyone. As someone once said, "Glad's dance card was always filled." With wavy jet-black hair and piercing, sparkly green eyes, she was a stunning fashion plate who loved the latest look and often modelled for a clothing house in the city. (In fact, I'm told that when she and my father went to a party, they had the aura of movie stars of the day.)

Glad's passion was the piano. Her deep red fingernails would fly across the keyboard and entertain party-goers in her home and throughout the city. She had trained in Winnipeg and later studied at the Royal Conservatory of Music in Toronto. Some say she was accomplished enough to have been a concert pianist. But her dreams lay away from that field. According to Dee, Glad wanted to be a fashion designer, but that was not yet an occupation for a young woman. Instead, she married my father and settled down to married life.

On the afternoon of December 6, Jack, my father, was in Calgary where he lived and worked. (He had allowed Glad to move home to Winnipeg several months before I was due because she was so lonely in Calgary.) I'm not certain what to tell you about this man. However, from Dee, I do know these three things: he adored my mother; he did not like Dee (but then she didn't like him!); and he was personable with people he wanted to impress. Although Dee had approved of the man my mother had intended to marry before she met my father, Dee respected Jack for, as she said, "his care of and love for my daughter."

How else can I describe him? Well, one thing I must tell you is that I'm his spitting image: facial features, shape of head, eyes, body build, fingernails, walk—all of it. And, I loathed this resemblance for many years. I wanted to look like a Little, my true family in my mind.

Jack was a very handsome, fair-haired man; his mother adored him because he was her one successful son, the son who did all the right things and acquired all the right possessions—to her, the marks of a "successful" man.

Jack was also an athlete and excelled at two sports. He was a scratch golfer, and in the true tradition of the times, he played third for the curling team out of the Strathcona Curling Club, which won the Manitoba Brier in the mid-1940s. His other passion, or vice, as Dee called it, was gambling, especially poker and snooker.

In the early 1940s, when I was still an infant, Jack returned from Calgary and joined the Manitoba Sugar Company. However, before he could settle into that job, he was seconded to a position at the War Time Price and Trades Board in Ottawa, where he oversaw sugar rationing during the latter part of the war. He lived in Ottawa during the week, returning to Winnipeg on weekends.

When Glad arrived at Dee's house on the eve of my birth, she expected also to see my Uncle Wib, who lived with Dee, but he was finishing up some chores at the Grain Exchange.

What a good-looker Wib was! He had dark wavy hair (just like Glad's) and a handsome face. One remarkable attribute was his eyelashes, which were the longest I've ever seen. His good looks were complemented by impeccably tailored suits that had a manful flair. He was a good man, always kind. He was also a ladies' man, very charming—and he knew it.

Wib had taken his schooling privately, later graduating from St. John's College at the University of Manitoba. He then took his father's seat at the Winnipeg Grain Exchange, a thriving institution that was the grain gateway of Western Canada.

I adored Wib. He could make thrilling shadow images of animals on a dimly lit wall. He read a great deal and his interests were wide and eclectic. A student of literature, he could quote Shakespeare and the Bible, verse upon verse. In a gathering, there was no finer conversationalist. Throughout his life, Wib was a person to whom I could say whatever came to mind.

Wib was a hero to me for many reasons, but he was an uncommon person too. He could spend hours alone with a book of poetry or a nineteenth-century novel. On the other hand, he always loved a party. The girls milled around and he was talented in the ways of keeping them entertained in a circle of interest.

When he was in his mid-thirties, staying at the family cottage for a weekend with Dee and me, Wib took a rescue trip in a fishing boat to free another boat from a rock. No one knows exactly how it happened but they needed to put down anchor, and in the process, Wib's left leg was caught in the rope. Later that terrible night, his leg was amputated just below the knee after he had suffered a painful ride back to Winnipeg. His life changed forever in that instant; he was grief-stricken for months.

Dee once talked about Wib's favourite gal, Daphne,

from Minneapolis, who must have been the light of his life. Soon after the amputation he was to tell her they could not marry, because he felt "half a man." He soldiered on with his life, living through the years with Dee, dying of a heart attack like his father, instantly, in the kitchen of his mother's house.

On the night of my birth, however, Wib was still healthy and happy. When my mother went into labour, he took her to the hospital and shepherded Dee about the halls through the waiting time. For that act, he was always my hero.

As for Aunt June, I never found out any details of her part in my birth day. At the time, she was eighteen years old, still living at home while completing her studies. However, it's unlikely that she would have been studying on a Sunday evening; more likely, she would have been visiting with a friend, or out on a date. The boys were fond of her with her beautiful blonde hair and her inviting, gentle green eyes.

As children, she and my mother had shared a bedroom even though my mother was six years older and the two were polar opposites: mother dark and quiet; June, fair with an engaging way about her. Dee told me nothing about June's early life. Nonetheless, June and I became closer when I was an adult and I loved her dearly.

Along with family members, Freda, Dee's maid, was also present that night in the great house at 890 Palmerston. Freda had been Dee's maid for two years at that point. A big-boned woman in her late twenties, Freda had left Germany before the war with her family. As so many immigrants did in those days, Freda's family settled on a farm in southwest Manitoba. But Freda wanted more. She had been a baker's assistant in a shop in Rothenberg, a beautiful old German city in Bavaria, which had an outer ring of stone walls. (I know this because I visited the city in the early 1970s.) When she came to my grandmother, she was a nervous young woman, but as time passed, she settled into 890. Her bedroom on the third floor was sparse (by choice), and dotted with photographs of her family and her dogs. Freda loved Dee and her children so much that she came to think of herself as almost a member of the family. That night, she was in the kitchen boiling a ham bone for soup, but she brought my grandmother tea when my grandmother rang for her.

Earlier that afternoon, Floyd, the handyman, had been busy at the house, shovelling snow as it fell along the snaky driveway, pausing in the midst of his labours to look longingly at his greenhouse packed on each side with hefty snow banks. He was a Scotsman from a village north of Dundee, where he had worked as an apprentice gardener on an estate called Eaglemere. (I've been there too, though now it's a shooting lodge.)

As well as working as a handyman, Floyd served as Dee's gardener. Of all the serving people in Dee's home in my very early years, I remember Floyd most clearly because he was my first friend. He was a small man, but strong; his hands were worn to a sandpaper-feel and smelled of the summer's earth; his eyes were wise, sky blue, and a bit rheumy.

In spring and early summer, I fancied myself as his helper because he gave me real (and, I thought, important) jobs in the garden or greenhouse. I was his shadow. I later realized that I loved Floyd for his infinite patience with me. Somehow he recognized his friendship was important to this child without playmates. The tricycle that Dee gave me had blocks built by Floyd on the pedals, all the better for fat little legs to reach. I skinned my knees frequently on the shale driveway and there he was, picking me up and getting me going again. Dare I say, Floyd was proud of my gumption.

Though I was rarely given the privilege of sharing morning coffee or afternoon tea with Floyd and Freda in the kitchen, Dee often told me what they talked about. That's one thing that I always admired about my grandmother. Through all the years I can remember, she enjoyed sitting with her help over a noontime meal that she sometimes made, while she heard their stories. It was that important to her, to know about their lives.

On the evening of December 6, the eve of my birth, Mrs. Quinn, who was to be my occasional babysitter, began working away with her knitting needles on another little outfit for me. (She was always knitting, and one of the few memories from my early childhood involves falling to sleep to the click of Mrs. Quinn's knitting needles.) She also sent her best black dress with a lace collar to be cleaned in anticipation of her upcoming babysitting assignment. Dee would talk about Mrs. Quinn with a tinge of admiration. After all, when Mrs. Quinn was employed to be my babysitter, she was in charge of "precious cargo" and had to keep up the storytelling, the mainstay of my wee life. She was a substantial woman, wide of girth, not fashionable, but certainly knowledgeable about other families for whom she sat. Stories did flow and when I repeated them for Dee, I was promptly told to forget them! Oh, yes! She played a mean game of checkers. I tell you about Mrs. Quinn because once I moved to be with my parents, I needed her to be my surrogate grandmother.

There is not much more that I can tell you about those who peopled my young life either before or after it began.

But what of my train? The caboose. Clickety Clack was silent and awaiting a delivery; the back brakeman and the conductor slept in their bunks. Little did they know that, soon, there would be a visitor.

……

The night of my birth was silent and snowy. On Sunday morning, December 7, 1939, just after midnight, I was born, weighing seven pounds, seven ounces. Immediately following my birth, I was taken to the nursery. Alone at the Winnipeg General Hospital, I was watched over by the nursing staff, but had no visitors.

The morning after my birth, my mother, feeling ill, did not see me. My father was in a different city. There was no entry in the yellow baby book. In fact there are no entries period. No day-of-birth photograph either.

I was an "accident" of nature; that's what I was told, without any explanation. Apparently my mother was not supposed to have had a baby. Later I became an "accident" of living: hereditary illness (manic depression) began with my first breath. It had struck my grandfather, his daughter June, and then me.

I have only snatches of memories until the age of twelve, most of them coming from Dee, but I have little understanding, even today, of many secrets.

I do, however, have one "secret" to tell you, a mystery solved in 2002. Why didn't I have any birthday parties until age twelve? I didn't get the story that explained the mystery from Dee; it came from another person who was part of the story itself.

Exactly five years before my birth, on December 7, 1934, Dee's husband, Harry Little, an expansive and moody man, had been buried at Elmwood Cemetery in Winnipeg. He had died at the age of forty-four in his lover's penthouse in Saskatoon. Draped in widow's weeds, Dorie, his paramour, had attended the committal and thrown herself on the coffin, before being whisked away to the train station for the return trip home. This was a bitter memory for Dee and her children. Though my mother, and later my father, would be buried in that plot, Dee, who outlived them both, did not get out of the limousine on either occasion to stand at the family grave site. She and June held hands and wept silently in the car, with the events of another day, long ago, seared in their memories.

As a result of this earlier event, December 7 was not a celebration of my birthday; it was a lonely, barren, miserable day, a day filled with sadness which I "felt" but could not know. I have only a few faded, unidentified childhood photographs in one album. Remember the baby book, given as a "shower gift," that was to be filled with notes and pictures? It's bare. Still empty at age sixty-nine.

......

DR. EDYE: Joy does not have many memories before the age of twelve, and when this is seen in an otherwise healthy person, it is a strong indication that there are painful memories being suppressed. Joy's sense of rejection at not warranting an entry in the baby book is still there sixty-nine years later. There were many harsh moments in Joy's childhood.

2 Shadows on the Walls

In this chapter I am a child, perhaps six years old. This is my first memory. I am caught in my bedclothes; the sheets are wrapped around me. I am hiding from the shadows I see on the wall outside my bedroom, a dark canvas of night-time images, products of a fierce imagination.

I am terrified. No one is at home. My parents are next door having cocktails, believing there is no need for a sitter. This memory, one of very few before the age of twelve, stands out because it is a harbinger of the rest of my childhood—a childhood filled with isolation, fear, and treachery, softened only by the love of my maternal grandmother, my uncle, Wib, and a few others, such as Haruko, the childhood nanny who replaced Mrs. Quinn.

You need to understand the importance of this memory. It is deeply imprinted; what and who I am today is very much a product of my experiences all those many years ago. Every stage of my life has had feelings of aloneness, of depersonalization, leading finally to the realization that I was a lost soul. My shadowy path can be seen in different hues, from pale grey to the pitch black of nothingness.

This is the beginning of the twists and turns of my Clickety Clack journey as I ride from age six into and out of the shadows. It's the beginning of sixty-nine years of striving to take control of my life.

Since then, I have lived my life as someone who needs a master to lead me through pitfalls and poor decisions; a perpetual child, I have frequently needed a patient "mother" to fix the scrapes and bruises and all the hurts of growing up, a daily job to keep me from myself, from drowning in my own "doings."

The discovery of the self, the answering of the question "Who am I?" was the clarion call for my fifties generation, and those on the heel of it. For most, it was a search to discover what those three words represented. For me, the words were a curse because there was never any resolution, never any answer. For me, the voyage of self-discovery has been just a circle back to point A. It has been a sometimes frightening journey, taken in order to love myself enough to weather my mistakes in judgment, my episodes of miscommunication, my failed personal relationships.

Often, I have faked bravado and confidence in order to manoeuvre a situation in hopes that it would work out. Whatever my state on a given day, I claimed that day as an outsider, on or off the rails.

The memory of these times began deep in early childhood, as I said, with me trapped in my bedclothes. Desperate to escape the shadows I felt threatening me, I crept to the entrance of my bedroom, knees weak from shaking. From there I began to make my way down the hall, along a narrow, gleaming hardwood floor, the walls painted with only a slight brush of stem green. The pull to travel from there to the kitchen, and maybe down the kitchen stairs to Haruko, was fierce, but the journey was daunting.

At the top of the hallway, just outside my bedroom, an old-fashioned linen closet was recessed into the wall. During idle afternoons, I often climbed up to the top shelf where I would find a bunch of love letters, tied with a maroon bow. They contained words that were unintelligible and unreadable for a six-year-old. They were a curiosity only, a secret—and what child can resist exploring that temptation? That evening, the familiar comfort of the linen closet offered a temporary way-station for me on my difficult journey downstairs.

Facing me at the other end of the hallway, which seemed a mile away, hung a painting of two pussycats, each with green bows, staring into the face of a frog as he sat on a rock in a stream. The title of the painting was *Who are You?* It hangs, still, in my writing studio above my desk, where I sit everyday. This kind of painting was to be found in every house I knew, maybe not with these pussycats, but certainly with bridges, stone houses, small villages, plains, hayfields, and hills, and all in old brass frames. Much later, I came to understand that this painting was like an old torch, flickering in a dusky night, a faint beacon that allowed me to master the hallway. Every child left alone needs safety and comfort—and I was about to begin the journey in search of them.

I felt that if I could run the gauntlet of the hallway from the cupboard to the pussycats, I would be safe. It might take an hour for my heart to resume its pace, but I would live to see another day. I was in anguish, my mind a whirlwind of images, shattered but smartly put into pigeonholes to use later—as ideas, for example, for my writing, which I began at an early age.

Sometimes, though, the wooden pigeonholes emptied in a flight of horror, like bats at night coming out of a tree in a frenzy. Images of animals and cruel creatures on the walls can do that when they grow and crawl along a wall. Light patterns become patterns of fright. The feelings and images of that night rolled around and became the sources of youthful nightmares and future psychoses.

A pounding heart, little feet running a race down a hall to my pussycats. Nobody there. Empty rooms. Doors locked. No arms to comfort. No "There, there, darling, Mommy will make it better. It's just a bad dream." They were not there. Just my shadows on the walls. Try making friends with these ever-changing figures on the wall? No. Too grotesque. Go to my bedroom closet and sit with my books, my friends, too? Hide away. Out of sight.

That's the way I looked at life from my bedroom. And, if in the night I needed to go to the kitchen—oh, boy! Scary, beyond words. But I could, I did, go with a dry mouth of fear.

Silly, this child's understanding of safety—two pussycats and Mr. Frog on the wall. Maybe that sounds funny. However, it was not a game then. It was dead serious. Here's why. There is nothing so unkind, so unfair, as to leave a child alone, confused and in bedclothes of fear. That hallway and its shadowy walls were my battlefield. It was where I fought the night-time shadows of frightening, oddly shaped creatures that vanquished a small soul.

My early experiences as a child whose parents were also "shadows on the walls" started my small life of abject loneliness. I was a prisoner. I had the courage to stand the night, but I did not feel brave. Where were they? Only next door, "having a drink and a night off." A night off from what? Me?

Should I tell the truth about "them," or are the secrets mine to keep? I think I will be brave. It's time.

……

DR. EDYE: Magical thinking—the belief that thoughts, words, or actions can cause or prevent events—is a normal phase of child development. Magical thinking also continues, though to a much lesser extent, in normal adulthood. If Joy ran as fast as she could to the pussycats, she would be safe. And that was her comfort, her way of coping with frightening loneliness.

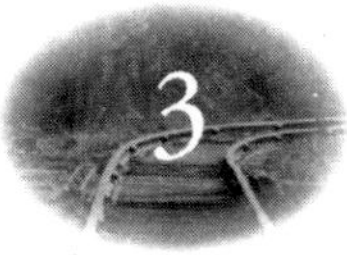

3 Hauntings

The child you see in this photograph is a lie. It is not the child I knew I was.

It haunted me then to think that I did (in this case, dressed) as I was told. Those actions did not square with my feelings about myself. It haunts now to realize that I was a pawn as well as a performer in a tableau of others' events and dreams.

When I was twelve, I became a poster child, dressed prettily in a red dress, new black patent leather shoes and a string of pearls. This was the "coming out" of a child of a prominent family, a family at the forefront of the political scene. But it was a haunting lie, an enormous insult to this child, who sensed deep to her core that this image was all wrong, that it needed to be erased to bring comfort to her world.

What is a "haunting"? Answer: A haunting is an activity or event that promotes guilt in me. I can be haunted by something I have done, something I couldn't help doing that

I know is not acceptable, either to me or to others. A haunting can also be caused by something that does not square with my self-image. For example, I cannot identify myself with the photograph. I should be in jeans, full of a rough-and-tumble attitude, throwing a ball, not a girl dressed like a doll on display—definitely not. The image tickled the edge of my gender confusion, even at a young age.

A haunting is something that sticks in my mind. It is tenacious and can cause an obsession-filled journey as I try to respond to it, as I try to confront, for example, an image that's out-of-place, or a harsh word, a glance of utter disapproval that assaults my self-image, a dagger of a rebuke regarding my dress, or lack of recognition for a job well done. There is no end to the list. I am never recognized and praised for who I really am.

The haunting hurts. Sometimes it hurts so much that it is not possible to find anything to alleviate the pain. The haunting scrapes my mind, wounding it, but then the scabs are ignored, because they are not seen, and I am left in confusion, with an overall feeling of inadequacy. I must jack myself up, again and again, by existing outside the haunting until the salve with which I treat my own wounds brings me back to the way I see myself. For instance, when trying to heal myself I'll often retreat into a book in a cozy space. I feel excitement at returning to myself.

Later, I came to learn that all hauntings are thoughts not allowed, under any circumstances, to surface to consciousness and become real—because I could not, dare not, give room to the pain, anger, and desperateness that they incite. Hauntings chip away inside but they also have a larger effect. I feel frail dealing with the world because it can trigger these thoughts. Writing about my hauntings now is difficult for me. I don't want to relive any of them, even on an intellectual level.

When I was a child, I didn't understand my hauntings. It seemed that they had no explanations. They made me squirm. They began to pile up during my childhood and eroded all my self-confidence, so that when I entered my teens, I was living in my own world while denying the presence of deep-seated unhappiness and brutal hurt. If nothing else, the effort of trying to deal with these hauntings taught me the art of compartmentalization: I carefully kept my feelings under wraps in order to get work done, or in my case, to live. (Clearly this narrowed my ability to cope with larger issues, but I always fell back on my pretend world where the pigeonhole compartments of the train's baggage car soothed the jangled self.)

One of the greatest and most poignant hauntings of my small life at the age of twelve was a birthday party at my house. It is an indelible memory because, incredibly, I have no memory of a previous birthday celebration. I know somehow that I never had one. Why? Do you suppose it was because of that unhappy memory of my maternal grandfather's burial? Or, was it because "they" dared not to care? Who will ever know? It was like so many other questions—greeted by silence.

Not only did I not have a yearly celebration of my birthday, I have no recollection of childhood friends in my house—another haunting. Yes, there were young callers, but when these friends rang the bell, they were forced to wait for me downstairs, in the tiled entranceway. None were invited to climb the stairs to our second-floor duplex. Only one, Janie, made it up the stairs. But she was never asked to stay, certainly not for a meal.

I had very few girlfriends. I had nothing in common with those who were not sports-minded. Those girlfriends I did have were faithful and true. In fact, Daphne and Diane (who are twins), and Janie and Gayle and I became "The Fearless Five," not to be messed with, and certainly loyal and protective of each other. We just had our fiftieth anniversary! But, as I said, no friends except Janie were ever, ever invited to my house for a visit; no one came for a meal. On the other hand, I would sometimes have dinner at Janie's, or play there on the third floor with her doctor-dad's war stuff.

And then I would ask myself, "Why?" Why couldn't friends—my best friends—come in to my house? You'd think my parents would have wanted to celebrate this close-knit substitute for a family. No. The house remained off-limits. It was as if it were a prison; no one had a "pass." Were my parents ashamed of me, of their house, and of their inability to talk to and interact with children? What was the matter? Another haunting.

It was in this time frame that I decided that not only was I not "significant" to my parents, but my friends were unwanted and therefore unworthy. These facts were the seed of many more hauntings in my life, each an indication of my decreasing sense of self-worth.

Sometimes my hauntings were a result of the fact that I asked a lot of questions of everyone in my life, even though occasionally I could not process the answer. My many unanswered questions would create confusion and anxiety, most especially in relation to my parents. I came to understand that they were the only people who did not respond to my need-to-know; nor did they seem to care enough that a haunting had created confusion and hurt.

Though I did not know then what I know now, to compensate for this void, I developed patterns of behaviour, such as deliberately challenging their instructions and their sense of what was proper, that relieved my feelings of unworthiness arising from constantly being dismissed from their thoughts, or from the room in which they had their secret whisperings.

Here's an example: I paraded the beach with bathing trunks (shorts) but would wear no top to cover my just-emerging breasts. Why? Well, why not? I was beginning to feel the "niggles" of gender confusion. But I was astute enough to see in my aunt's eyes that she was uncomfortable with this lack of decorum. So I had to squish the sense of inappropriateness into a box lest it mature into an obsession.

At the same time, I began to acquire—because I insisted on wearing boys' clothing—canoe shoes, a duffel coat, jeans, and tartan shirts. When my parents were gone from the house, I would dress up in my father's white shirt, tying a neat knot in my favourite of his ties. From the memory of piano music I had heard my mother play at parties, I would conduct a full orchestra in the mirror, always to great applause from the audience on the other side of the mirror. During these play sessions, I was able to indulge my love for my mother's music and my delight in dressing up in a way that felt comfortable.

These activities distressed my parents, causing many scenes; when I started to push things further, however, things became much more serious. Nineteen-fifty was the year of the Great Flood in Manitoba, when the city of Winnipeg was deluged with high waters by two rivers. Many children went to relatives out-of-province because of the fear of contaminated water in basements and around buildings. I was shipped off to my Aunt Marguerite in Toronto to finish out my school year. There I played with her two sons and their friends. Nothing pleased me more because it was all boys' stuff and games. And, strangely, I did not feel guilty.

I came home months later a changed child. More assertive, more sure of myself, more boyish: a boy in my head. This caused fear in my parents' eyes and demeanour. They reacted with disapproval and once again I felt "little" and ashamed. And the guilt came back. Another haunting.

In retaliation against my parents' disapproval, I began to act out further. I screamed obscenities out the window of a car being driven by the mother of my friend, Susan. Of course, I had to phone her mother to apologize. Uncontrollable anger had surfaced about many things in my life, including presumed "wrongs" done to me by other people.

One evening when my father came home from the office, expecting his perfect wife to be ready for cocktails, I got really angry at him. No particular reason. Just hugely angry. He had his socks off. I leaned over and chomped down on his big toe, drawing blood. He yelled and grabbed me, took off my sock and bit my big toe. First time I remember him asserting fatherly action. Tell you what. It cured me of biting.

Another example: I put my fist through the glass of the back door of my house because my mother would not let me in. Why so much anger? Easy answer. I was coming into my own personality with its side-kicks: strength of voice and a gender identity considerably different than the expectation of my parents, who demanded the clear image of the young girl in the red dress and pearls seen in the photograph. I was to be the fair-haired, blue-eyed child of good looks, gaiety, and charm. Not any other strongly developing child.

Life continued in my lane, not theirs.

"Don't play with matches." I did, causing a garage fire. "Don't turn that bike upside down and turn the peddles." I did. Then I stuck my index finger in to stop the motion; it came off and had to be re-attached to my hand. "Don't walk along that fence." I did, and broke my arm. I was angry, and now I had become defiant.

"No, you cannot have that camera at the hardware store. No, you cannot get that baseball glove." I lusted after both, going everyday to see if they were still waiting for only me. "You want to do what? NO! Under no circumstances can you have a paper route." I got the camera and the baseball glove by cutting grass for the Hurleys next door and doing odd jobs for my grandmother; the paper route was a little more difficult. I got Patrick, my other next-door neighbour, to put the route in his name and we did papers together, he of course delivering to my house.

Where there is the will of a stubborn child, there's always a way! Each item, but most especially the baseball mitt, was a necessity. Because I played sandlot baseball at Grosvenor School—and truthfully I was the best, with the longest throw—I needed to look the part of a pro, to be a regular guy.

A few Sunday mornings I went with my dad to the sugar refinery, where he was general manager. For two reasons: I wanted to walk through the refinery and enjoy the smell of molasses, and I wanted to talk to the guys, who were always willing to patiently explain the various processes, over and over again. I hoped to get a summer job someday bagging sugar because it was a manly job. I was ready to work.

Also, I wanted to go to Gib's office. He was the accountant. His desk held treasures—paper and dozens of pencils. I would sharpen, say, a dozen pencils, line them up carefully and evenly, then begin writing, about anything. At the end of my session, I'd sharpen the pencils and put them neatly back in the drawer. I dreamed of writing. I longed (while staring out the window toward the refinery) of writing and never stopping, of being in my own world where I controlled my own paper and pencils, and where I would have a never-ending supply of both. They would be mine. Why? Because that's where my heart went: fighting against the attempt to turn me into a little lady.

To escape the disapproval of my parents I would visit with Grandma Dee. She approved of me, totally, and what's more, she showed it in deed and word. Dee would listen to my stories, all of them. She knew the names of my friends. She knew their parents and grandparents. She would tell me about her horse, Danny Boy, about riding in the bush with friends, about going overseas with Uncle Wib and my mother, Glad, when they were small. Always to Scotland, where Dee would visit Grandpa Harry's mother and sisters, to whom she remained close and whom she supported when they were widowed. Dee would talk about the early days of arriving by ship, after motion sickness the entire voyage.

She told me about going to a London hotel, and in the evening, getting dressed in a long gown to go to the West End theatres for a show. She and Harry would arrive early so they could see others arriving and admire the fashions.

Grandma Dee and me

I expect Dee shopped at Harrod's because she was always dressed in the fashion of the times.

On several occasions she would tell me stories about shopping in Paris. For her, the trip over from England to France was frightening because people on board the "flying machine" had to wear what approximated a gas mask for oxygen!

Though both my parents' home and Dee's were beautifully appointed, Dee's was inviting, gentle, warm, and loving. Mine was agitated, cold, and eerily silent. I remember bounding into my house and up the gleaming staircase, then being gripped by fear, anticipating a disapproving voice over something I had or hadn't done. My house was not a home for the living, and my loving came from the outside. Why?

I learned early that the only place I felt I could be myself was alone with my Dee at the beach. I played all day with my friend Kit. (We even rode in the train's cowcatcher to the wye for a turnabout.) At night I was cozy by a fire talking to Dee. And I slept tight, secure, with no fear. (Dee's two yellow canaries had hoods on their cages and so they slept securely, too!)

I did try to lead my own life at home though, too, difficult as that was. There was a sandbox at Patrick's. The guys would go there to play with dinky toys. So did I—with their toys. But, at home, I was told, "No, you can't have a train car. Those are for boys."

Freddie, one of the neighbourhood boys, had a train. His dad had set it up in his basement on a ping-pong table. Thinking back, it was a beauty. A long train that could go over hills, under bridges, through mountains, and around and around. "May I have a train for my basement?" No. Why?

Many years later, when talking to my friend and confidante Elaine about the missed events of our small lives, I told her how much I had always longed for a long miniature train. Guess what? While staying with them for Christmas when I was forty, my friend Ross, Elaine's husband, worked all Christmas Eve setting up a train that went through their family room—and I was as excited as a child in the morning. Disbelief and awe. Finally. So there!

I have books on trains, too. Thus began my life-long fascination with trains, and in particular, the Clickety Clack caboose where I could fly in my imagination to safety from chaos.

As a child, I also read the Hardy Boys books; the girls read Nancy Drew mysteries. I read comic books for boys. I imitated most of the attributes of boys, and the feelings that resulted left me, at best, thrilled, and at worst, guilt-ridden.

Although the subject was never discussed, I knew I was not simply a tom-boy. I suspect my parents did too. Not only did I dress in a more masculine fashion, I had the mannerisms to match. My dress and mannerisms sometimes resulted in me being confused for a boy in a public bathroom. While my gender confusion caused me to dress and act as I did, my actions and dress also resulted in confusion by women in the bathroom. They took me for a male and were flustered. Another haunting.

The only person who would let me know I had a boundary was my grandmother; she did this especially when she was having her friends over for bridge and tea.

......

In and around my twelfth year, I discovered that a car was a freedom machine. I learned to drive the car sitting in Dee's lap. Why didn't my father take on that parental job? When he didn't and I realized that I could not be driving with Dee every day, I had a thought: "You are a good driver. You love the feel of the wheel. Why not drive yourself?" This led to another haunting.

In our garage, I could get lost for hours sitting in my mother's Morris Mini, pretending that I was doing errands or going to the park like Dee did. I imagined the roads I had gone down with Dee; I could picture them perfectly. I'm sure I wore out the clutch and gearbox. It didn't matter. I was free. That feeling of the open road carried on into adulthood when I drove, first, my MGB, and later a Mercedes roadster, before settling in at sixty to a big SUV, big enough to be king of the road. Why didn't my father teach me to drive?

Earlier, my grandmother had also taught me to ride my three-wheel bike. Many times I skinned my knees on the gravel of her driveway. And many times she or Floyd, the gardener, picked me up. I was undaunted in learning the workings of things that moved and could set me free. I was obsessed with freedom because I had so little of it.

Mother didn't go many places in the day except occasionally to her Guild and to play golf. In fact, she had only four or five good friends that I knew of during all my childhood. Why didn't my mother go out and be social like other mothers? (Years later, someone described my mother as an "ethereal wisp of a woman dressed in pastel colours who floated through her life.")

I longed for time alone with my mom. However, my father was always there. There was no opportunity to tell her my things, thoughts, feelings, happenings. I was made more lonely because my father stood in the way. What I remember most was the fear and aloneness when my mother had gallbladder surgery. She was confined afterward for over two weeks, and as many times as I asked, I was not allowed to see her until one day she came out in her housecoat. Why?

I liked my friends' mothers. They were very good to me. I liked sitting at the Smith breakfast table and eating crisp bacon with the twins before their dad drove us to school. I liked sitting at their dining room table, listening to everyone talking. I felt included, almost a member of the family.

When we went occasionally for Sunday dinner at Dee's, no one talked about anything worthwhile. It appeared to me that we were there because we had to be. It was awkward for Dee and I was sad for her, because she, too, had difficulty in seeing and talking to her daughter. My father was always in the way. So we rushed through dinner to get home—and be silent again. It was a stifling silence, the kind that you want to fill up, if possible, with something significant. But there was nothing I could do. I knew that I wasn't significant to them, and that they preferred silence following the negative energy my father displayed at Dee's, a place he couldn't bear. Why?

On rare occasions when my parents had a party, my mother played the piano. The music thrilled my ears and all of me! I wanted to listen, but was not allowed. Why? When there was a party at my friends' homes, the children always could come into the room.

I felt so unloved. I hungered for my mother, and because she was out of my reach and protected from me by my father, I hungered for many mothers. I wanted a million hugs, a million stories, a billion affirmations—"I love you; you're a good girl."

To fill my loneliness, I read, constantly. There was life in stories. I went to the library often. No one told me what to read. I found what I wanted. Apparently I forgot to get nursery rhymes, because in my fifties, friends, whom I had told about "my lack of education" in nursery rhymes, gave me the most exceptional illustrated fairy-tale books. Another haunting, a big one. Where was my mother when I was a child? I needed to hear her soothing voice, but I rarely did, under any circumstance. Why?

The whys are legion. You've read of many. And there are more and more. Always, the answers are few, or maybe incorrect. Never, ever, did I understand my parents, what they might think about any issue, activity, occurrence... anything.

Here's what I have learned, and what I think in my heart. Home was a place where three people lived; only two were welcome there, though. I was not an integral part of my parents' lives. Either they didn't know how to include me in their lives, or they didn't care to make me a part of them. I was excluded, perhaps not intentionally, but perhaps because I was "too much to handle." High-spirited. Demanding. Boisterous. Easily angered. Aggressive. Unladylike. Not interested in girl-type activities or dressing. Worst of all, I had dreams beyond the white picket fence and the husband who came home to his perfect wife and children. Sorry! My life was going to be bigger!

The whys then turned into hauntings. Above all, I was haunted by why my parents chose not to love me. Perhaps they did, but there was never any demonstration of it, save the provision of a house, food, clothes, and schooling. I am convinced that I was a bother in what was to be a two-person family only. I seemed to rip at that bond. I was in the way.

It's as if they walked through my life and out the other side without seeing me. I was their ghost child. In one of the only pictures of me from my childhood, I seem to be there in body but not in spirit. In the photo, I am dressed in a coat with fur collar and matching hat and gloves beside a big car at the city park. I look so sad. Why? And why are there no other photos of childhood events, or family pictures? Was I bad? Or were there no happy occasions? I don't know; I can't remember any.

......

I have referred earlier in this chapter to the pigeonholes of the train's baggage car, where I stored my hauntings. Thankfully, somewhere around age eight, my mind created the Clickety Clack train to deal with these hauntings. The idea of the train and my friends in the caboose came from love of travelling to and from the family's summer cottage at Victoria Beach. As soon as we boarded the train, I knew I was safe and loved. I came to associate the train with overwhelming calm, peace, and the anticipation of spending time in the quiet of my grandmother's presence.

I knew the structure of a train. I had learned it by following the conductor in his travels through the cars (without, I may add, any instruction to the contrary from my grandmother, who remained in her seat). I asked the conductor to tell me about the "cars" that he said I couldn't see.

Finally, I decided that the structure of "my train" would have just the caboose and the box car forward of it. Into that box car my mind would jump, then turn immediately right. In front of me, from floor to ceiling, was a wall with, oh, maybe 200 pigeonhole boxes, much like you'd find in a post office. Into each pigeonhole, usually on a nightly basis, I would put any "haunting" that may have troubled me. Once a feeling of unworthiness or any other baggage that caused unnerving dismay had been "stored," I would happily skip off to the caboose and into the safe and loving protection of Ernie and Mr. McTavish.

I was a day-dreamer. I needed a magical tranquilizer and that's what Clickety Clack became. It was my "night train," an extension of the real train that took me to the beach. I always knew when it was time to go to the caboose. I would experience difficulty falling asleep, or I would be worried and tense. It was time to "magically" put myself into the boxcar to lose the thoughts that had to be lost and then move into the caboose to say hello to Ernie and Mr. McTavish, who were both pleased as punch to have me there for company. Each treated me as a child needing their attention. Most of all, they knew I needed the safety of a familiar magical place. I had part of Mr. McTavish's bench to sit on; Ernie put up the tea; and I would hear stories of the day and imagine being whisked down the track to some place new with each journey. It was exciting. I listened in my mind to the "clickety clack, clickety clack" on the rails, while my mind "went off the rails" and into some trance-like state of complete make-believe.

I was happy in the caboose and as the years went along, I went to the caboose often. Later, I'll tell you more about these nocturnal visits, which I still make, because the caboose is the one place where there are no hauntings.

......

DR. EDYE: Joy describes feeling much more comfortable in "boys' clothes," an early realization that she could not tolerate stereotypical girls' dress and playtime activities. She wanted to be athletic and strong. She visualized being male, doing a traditionally male job (such as bagging sugar or serving as the conductor of the Bipolar Express, or her two magical friends' jobs).

Joy's need to line up and sharpen pencils suggests she is developing obsessions and compulsions. An obsession is a persistent, unwelcome, and uncontrollable thought or feeling. Common ones include fear of something happening to a loved one, or an excessive need to do everything perfectly. A compulsion is an irresistible repetitive impulse to act. The most common one is washing or cleaning.

The most reliable and supportive men in her life were her imaginary companions. About this time, Joy is wilfully disobeying orders—engaging in defiant behaviour. She is angry and it is obvious. There may have been many causes for her anger, some from rebellion against rejection and invisibility.

"Lieutenant Governor J.S. McDiarmid and Mrs. McDiarmid gave their patronage to the gala opening of the Royal Winnipeg Ballet, held Monday at the Playhouse Theatre. On the left is His Honor's aide de camp, Lt. Cmdr. L.E. Avery and Miss Evelyn Scott; on the right, Miss Joy McDiarmid, granddaughter of Mr. and Mrs. McDiarmid."

PHOTO AND CAPTION FROM THE *WINNIPEG FREE PRESS*

4 *The Queen is Coming...*

The story that follows captures the reality of my teen years, years for which I was ill-equipped, mentally and emotionally. The setting is Government House in Winnipeg, Manitoba, which was the home of my paternal grandparents. The house is imposing, nestled in trees near the bank of the Assiniboine River across from the Manitoba Legislature. This place was my nemesis for six years, 1953 to 1959.

There was enough anguish in my young life without being subjected to the pressures of privilege, prominence, and performance that went along with life in Government House. I was out of my element, but there was no escape. The energy I expended to deal with these pressures would affect me for the rest of my life. There is no therapy for a child thrust unwillingly into the limelight.

The double-glass doors to the front door opened effortlessly. In I walked and stopped. Oh, dear! The vast blue rug that ran the entire lobby and into every nook and cranny of this entrance was smooth. A footprint would not be "right" because the pile had been hoovered so that it stood perfectly vertical. I looked for another path—in vain. So on I moved, feet lightly touching the edges of the broadloom.

Looking around, I could see that the mahogany tables, four of them, gleamed with fresh polish. One large table at the top of the entrance was stunning. A gigantic alabaster-coloured jug with Grecian handles sat in the centre, spilling forth more than a dozen chrysanthemums, whose blooms of pure white accented their green stems. The arrangement was reflected in an oblong mirror with a gilt-edge frame, truly a magnificent sight. I felt overwhelmed and yet proud that this house, where my paternal grandparents lived, was so beautiful and grand.

I stood to catch my breath, as I always needed to do coming into that house. I looked right, into the drawing room. Then, left to the dining room. No Gran. Most likely, she was upstairs in the library, which also served as her office.

Gran was Gertrude McDiarmid. She was the chatelaine, or hostess, of Manitoba's Government House. My grandfather, John Stewart McDiarmid, was the province's lieutenant governor, the top dog. This post was a patronage appointment for a "job well done" in politics. He had been a Member of Parliament in Ottawa and later minister of mines and natural resources for the province. Politics had been his life, but he was more than a politician. He was a diplomat in the true sense of the word, a gentleman of the highest order, and thus truly a natural in his role as the Queen's representative in the province.

The date was July 1959. Her Majesty Queen Elizabeth II and His Royal Highness Prince Philip were on a Canada-wide tour that brought them to Winnipeg to attend the grand opening of the Winnipeg Ballet Company. Their visit began with a smashing dinner at Government House.

McDiarmid family albums abound with photographs taken before, during, and after this event, as well as many others. In fact, the official photographer never got tired of photographing me, in all my activities: standing at the door, presenting flowers, sitting at the ballet, and saying good night. My mother was his second-favourite subject. And, on this occasion, he was doubly enamoured of her, because her long dress was only slightly different than the Queen's, a coincidence which stunned my grandmother.

Of course, there were many other visits and events. Most notably, afternoon teas and receptions, but also the state visits of the Right Honourable Vincent Massey, the governor general of the time, and Princess Mary, sister of the Queen's father.

How did these years in the public spotlight affect this child who was beginning to blossom?

Let's begin with my grandmother. As a hostess, no one was finer; she had a flair for making this large home welcoming to all those who crossed the front door. However, she could also be pompous and demanding. She had a way of rankling people not of her "station," especially the kitchen and serving staff. (I took this behaviour personally because it embarrassed me, but mostly because the staff members were "friends" of mine, since I worked with them from one event to the other.) Gran's negative side had a tremendous impact on my psychic health. Since I was the oldest female grandchild, she absolutely insisted that I partake in public ceremonies at the residence. By overwhelming me with duties that I was not happy performing, and

Left to right: My father, John Stewart McDiarmid, Jr.; his father, Lieutenant Governor J.S. McDiarmid; Her Majesty Queen Elizabeth II; and His Royal Highness Prince Philip, to whom my mother, Glad, curtsies.

forcing me into situations where I was utterly uncomfortable, she undermined my emotional stability. This undercurrent, joined with a number of experiences that affected me adversely at Government House, put a black spot on those years.

Even before the McDiarmids took up residence at Government House in 1953, Gran often used me to present bouquets of flowers to dignitaries and members of Britain's royal household when they were visiting the province. I would inevitably be specially outfitted in a smocked dress with matching coloured bow in my very blonde hair, so that I would look presentable. I would also be pressed into helping my grandmother with her duties as hostess when some of these people stayed in house. However, regardless of the circumstances, I was always a nervous wreck.

The teen years are delicate for a person. I was resentful of having to be back in my parents' house at a certain time. "You need to go to bed early so you will be bright for tomorrow's event," my mother would say. (Hard to tell a date that you had to be home at 10:00 p.m., or at midnight on New Year's Eve, because of the big party at the house on New Year's Day.)

Then there was all the chatter and fussing and fuming over clothes. I wanted to be in my rough-and-tumble stuff to the very last minute before changing into my "appropriate" clothes. I would do most anything to postpone the agony of dressing up. To make things worse, I was always to'ing and fro'ing from our seamstress, Madame Ringrose, who either made or fixed what I wore to each event. This was work, hard work; I had to stay perfectly still while she stuck a pin here or there to shorten a dress or change its look.

At the same time, the status of being part of the household separated me from some of my friends. They avoided me because they thought I might become "hoity-toity," even though I made sure that never happened. For example, when I had to stay at the house and the chauffeur would drive me to school, I would always have him let me off a block from school so I could walk the rest of the way. No showing off was my credo for six years.

Before any tea party, the tasks were endless. I had to fill the cigarette and matches holders, and meet with my grandmother to listen to the list of guests so that I would be familiar with who was coming, all the better to call each person by name. (I developed a system of letters to remember names.) Next, I was to say hello to Mrs. Black and her "girls" in the kitchen, and tell them who would be pouring the tea and who the coffee. Then I was to get a fresh white guest book, affix a copy of the official guest list to the left-hand side of the first page. Once the book was set at the proper angle for signing a page, I also angled the chair with its petit-point cover, to make a person comfortable. The final task was to get out a fresh pen with the engraved crest of Government House from the drawer and put it in the fold of the book.

That done, I was "officially on duty," ready to greet some of the early "players" in an event: the military aides-de-camp from the air force, army, and navy with their dress uniforms sparkling with medals, and the civilian aide-de-camp, who was my father, resplendent in dress clothes, the choice of which depended on the time of the event (for dinner, a white jacket, black cummerbund, black bow tie, and pocket handkerchief; for a Speech from the Throne, tails, grey vest and tie, and grey-striped pants).

My grandmother chose people from her list of favourite friends, along with their daughters, to serve sandwiches and cake and pour tea. Once this contingent had arrived and were stationed as they should be, I returned to the front door with the navy aide, who not only greeted guests with me, but showed the men to the cloakroom and the ladies up the grand staircase into a guest room where they "dropped their furs." Oh me, oh my! Such a to-do!

I am sure any child with confidence would have loved the experience, but for me, it was hard to handle. My social phobia, my fright of "important" people, my gender issues (more about that in the next chapter) and, of course, the fuss of worrying about proper dressing and manners made it all a great deal of hard work. I was so worn out from each effort that I never looked forward to an event. Of course, I should add that I faked each happening with the aplomb of a pro! (After all, I had been trained from my earliest years to understand the importance of observing decorum, not to mention the importance of doing nothing to shame the family name.)

I soon learned the best place to be, after I had completed my early duties, was the kitchen pantry, where Mrs. Black, who knew what a scaredy-cat I really was, let me hide among the many long trays of sandwiches and dainties for the tea table. My favourite was the row upon row of chocolate squares. I would have a tummy ache the next day, but at least I was safe for the rest of the party! Sometimes I would ride my grandfather's private elevator from the cloakroom to his bedroom and sit with his books.

It seems so long ago as I write now; however, it was traumatic. I had perpetual tummy aches, and not just from the cookies and cakes! I can still taste the dryness, the anxiety in my throat. I feel as frightened today as I was then.

I had three "rewards" for these six years: a barium test that revealed one big fat ulcer, low self-esteem, and guilt, all of which remained with me for years. You may be interested to know that in a move ten years ago, I pitched out all the photographs of those years, save four: one of my father leaning over the Queen while she signed the guest register; one of my mother, looking gorgeous, curtsying to Prince Phillip; and two of me. In one, I'm wearing a red dress with pearls, and in the other, I'm playing with a child's tea set. Nothing more than these reminders are necessary.

However, I must confess that I had a bounce to my step while in Government House, which I presume came from my overly active, energetic, inquisitive self. I was intrigued by the people who came to visit, so I tried to conquer my other natural tendency, which was to fear social experiences.

Social phobia and its sidekick, anxiety, were overwhelming during those years. After an event, in bed in the quiet of the night, I spent time with Ernie and Mr. McTavish; I had so much to say and so much advice and reassurance to ask for. I was needy.

This is where I needed to be. This was my caboose—a warm and safe place where I could visit two adult friends who loved me and wanted nothing but my company while we had a good wag over a cup of tea with lots of milk and sugar.

I was home.

......

DR. EDYE: Rules and fears. Joy writes about being a "poster child" with all the rules that accompany this role. Being the centre of attention was stressful: Joy wanted to please her family; she felt peer pressure to be unchanged and ordinary; and perhaps above all, she had to cope with the discomfort of having to meet traditional female stereotypes.

5 Gender Identity

In those heady days at Government House, I was assaulted by a social phobia edged by unmanageable anxiety. Yet, I bent to the awesome will of Grandmother McDiarmid; as chatelaine, she had enormous social skills, not to mention unrelenting persuasion.

However, after years of rising to occasions and then recovering from them, I was exhausted. The discord between what I knew I was and what I was asked to be became unbearable. I needed to be alone. I needed to crawl into a place where I could feel secure, where issues of image and self-perception could not reach me.

And that is exactly what I did. I withdrew. And in that moment, I knew I would fall apart and Humpty Dumpty would not be put back together again, at least not for a long time. I was in hell.

I was no dummy, but being uneducated in matters of the psyche, I didn't think I needed professional help. But my depression deepened to the point where I hid in my bed. Anxiety-ridden and afraid to leave the house, I found myself at the bottom of a big black hole. Only then did I run to my mother to confess how physically and mentally sick I felt. Of course, I knew she would tell my father, and then, to put it bluntly, the shit would hit the fan.

He wouldn't stand for me "bothering" my mother; he said that I needed help—he'd fix it. Later that day, I was sent to a psychiatrist whom I knew from my parents' cocktail circuit.

What did I know about psychiatry? When I was fifteen, all my ills had usually been "fixed" by a general practitioner, or GP, including my original diagnosis of manic depression (now known as bipolar disorder). I learned, much later, that this diagnosis was based only on the fact that my aunt, who was also his patient, was fully manic depressive.

At nineteen years old, however, entering third year university, I needed more help than ever. Two years earlier I had enrolled at the University of Manitoba, and I was now struggling to complete my Bachelor of Arts degree. The stress of my studies combined with the much greater stress of playing the role demanded by my family caused a breakdown. I couldn't cope, and to protect myself, I withdrew. I felt like my life was over.

The psychiatrist I was sent to see did nothing to relieve this feeling. I liked him; he was kind. But he said nothing that helped the panic and fear that were choking me. He was not suited to guiding a young person. However, with him, I began the longest journey of my life. For the next forty years, I would work with three psychiatrists and a GP, examining various theories about discord relating to gender and sexuality, bipolar disorder, and a number of related difficulties.

Government House had brought me to my knees. It had

forced me to begin a struggle (read "war"), lasting almost a lifetime, to come to grips with these issues, in all their aspects.

You see, I believe that my depression started in early childhood, and grew exponentially as the years passed. The "remedy" for the depression in these years and up to my teens was activity and sports. When my sports "career" was on the wane, my first psychiatrist started an experimental drug, Parnate, one of the few drugs available at the time to ameliorate depression. This drug failed me, some time in 1960. (Parnate is now not recommended for children, adolescents, or young adults since it has been shown to increase the risk of suicidal behaviour in those groups.)

While my depression was not something my parents were comfortable with, the fact that my aunt had also been diagnosed as depressive made this component of my mental disorders more or less "acceptable"; my gender identity (sometimes called gender confusion or gender discord) issues, however, were viewed very negatively by my parents. Their disapproval mounted as I grew older and was expected more and more to behave like "a young lady."

Somehow, despite all of this, I managed to graduate from university. Once I graduated and began to work, however, the expectations became even greater. In those days women were expected to "dress appropriately," meaning in a feminine fashion. The stress of dealing with these issues, with everyone's expectations and with my parents' disapproval, took out all my stuffing.

It has taken me many years to reach a point where I am able to deal with these issues with any measure of ease, but in those days, when I was trying to act a role, each day was a struggle. Let me explain.

At the start of each morning, I would be in a complete panic. I had an outright war between my selves, between my identities. Female? Male? What to wear? I had to make a selection of the appropriate clothes—appropriate to the day ahead's events, and suitable to whichever identity was in the ascendant that day. If I dressed appropriately, then I was able to function smoothly, and I would have less guilt, and less depression. So, I had two clothes cupboards: one for work, conservative and smart; and one for my time, comfortable and obviously more mannish. I dressed to suit my mood, even for work. This conflict extended everywhere, whether I was walking down the street, or lying on the beach in the summertime. I wanted to look like (be) a young man, with a super physique and smart clothes.

Was I a cross-dresser? No. In my younger years, I enjoyed getting all gussied up for a party, complete with make-up and jewellery, even though this also brought on anxieties about identity. I enjoyed a party and all the frivolity that went with that lifestyle. Was it a cover-up? No, it was me, then. But after the lid on my gender identity was blown completely off, that ability to shift to "dress-up" clothes was lost. Thereafter, when the occasion demanded "womanly" dress clothes, I did the best I could to look the part, but increasingly I felt that I could no longer lead a double life.

In the morning, my heart would rev up when I looked in the mirror to decide whether I appeared "appropriate." This was scary because then I had to decide: Am I a woman? Am I a man? Who am I? No answer. The mirror was my nemesis. So I'd make a blind choice on clothes and get into the day. Do something, anything, to make me calm, or at least settled enough to work.

Always I needed to remember that these loaded words,

identity and suitability, scary as they were, governed how the day would go. I tried to avoid situations that might exacerbate feelings of confusion, either in me or in others, such as, for example, the possibility of a gas attendant calling me "sir," a telephone surveyor grilling me as a man, a person on the street needing to look twice to see whether I was a man or a woman, or, worst of all, a friend or colleague being made to feel uncomfortable because I seemed to be playing with gender roles. Always, I could see it in their eyes. If I wore lipstick, I would only get a stare, but a "knowing" one.

It still happens, a dozen times a day when I'm dressed in "comfort" clothes. People have expectations. If you don't fit the mould, you can be cast out—in any situation. You become the proverbial wallflower at a dance. These feelings last a lifetime. You want to scream, "I'm a good person, too!"

My gender identity issues have caused me many problems over the years. For example, I seemed to want to head to the men's public washroom. This scared me but not near as much as going to the woman's bathroom, and feeling that I should stand up to pee. It's better today than it was forty years ago, but occasionally it happens, and I am as paralyzed now as I was in the beginning.

I also worried every day that I might say something male-oriented. Say, at coffee time at my university work, I would think, what if someone heard me? I'd shake. My knees would go weak. I couldn't blow my cover. I didn't want to reveal my story, so I was forever on watch.

On balance, not all of my twenties and thirties were traumatic. Yes, every day I had clothing decisions to make, but once I knew clearly my identity of the day, I went forward. It's stunning to me now that I didn't know I was in a serious and potentially dangerous psychiatric condition. As far as I was concerned I had a "loose" and floating identity.

Things finally came to a head, however, one ordinary day in the winter of 1978: I collapsed in the kitchen of my apartment while making my breakfast. I was suffering from severe depression at the time, having recently suffered the loss of both my parents and my beloved grandmother, Dee. Somehow I managed to get myself going and go off to work but I couldn't really function any longer; I couldn't play the game any more. I needed help.

The next day I called my Aunt June, the one with manic depression. She came. We went to the emergency department of a local hospital, where she had a prearranged visit with a psychiatrist. He helped to lift some of the fear I was feeling and dispensed some medication. Then, what? I don't remember...oh yes I do: ECT. He had me committed and I was subjected to three months of electroconvulsive therapy treatments.

These treatments helped to stabilize me but they did nothing to help me face the profound gender and sexual identity issues that now seemed to occupy my every waking hour. The treatments interrupted the steady flow of my life, but then, later, at night, these twin marauders took control of my life completely. I was no longer the blue-eyed, blonde-haired young woman who had been on display at Government House. People may have suspected that I was someone else but no one knew. I had carried my life in a suitcase, held only by me, until the early 2000s when I finally wrote this book and revealed my struggle to escape from never-never land.

I want to be clear: I know now that my body is that of a woman; but I also know my brain is made up of male thoughts and perspectives. I am sixty percent male, forty percent female. I am not a lesbian; I am not bisexual; I am not transgendered; I am not transsexual; I am not a cross-dresser. I have worked out my own formula with my psychiatrist. And this gives me the licence to say unequivocally that I am male enough to be attracted to women. This is all uncomfortable for me because I have a terrible, worrisome, anxious response inside me to all those words. I am not judgmental, and completely support the choice of others to identify themselves using any of the terms I listed above. Perhaps I could be accused of keeping my head in the sand, but I find that I am simply more comfortable without labels. I function to a higher degree, believing that I am unique, as is everyone. And, if this "no-name" label is my form of self-acceptance, so be it.

I did not have a bona fide diagnosis of "gender identity discord/confusion" from a psychiatrist until I was in my sixties, although I had already deduced it for myself in my mid-twenties. For years, I had asked questions but did not get the real answers. The only answer in those days was, "You are ahead of your times in attitudes and dress."

I so badly didn't want to be a transsexual and now I know that I'm not. My life has been split between what I am (female) and what I feel I am (more male than female). It's a question of body versus brain. So, in the end, my core sense of self was affected for forty-odd years until I had that final diagnosis and explanation of who and what I am.

I never considered having surgery to become transgendered; however, at the same time, I can't say that I'm "attached" to my female organs and breasts. I am amazed sometimes that I have them! I am in awe of those who have had the surgery. For me, there was no need for it. And, in any event, I wouldn't have had it for other reasons: a lack of opportunity and courage; and the consequences, given the high profile of my family. I know I would have become an outcast from those I loved. Maintaining my body as it is was important to me.

I do regret not having had the opportunity to talk to someone who is transgendered. I was curious and wanted to hear the stories that such a person could tell. I am certain I would have learned so much that would have made life easier and the future brighter. Besides, it would have been good to have a "real friend." That said, I hope young people today, grappling with gender identity issues, pursue the opportunity to talk to a resource person or someone with similar issues.

My generation was frozen in its inability to countenance anything "different" and therefore we were the "guilt generation." Who could I have told? Where would one go to get help? I was lost in a maze and so alone.

But I had hope that I would find my way. And then hope became real help. Some twenty-five years later, after the retirement of Dr. Don Rodgers, my second psychiatrist, I began to work with Dr. Frances Edye. She can whittle the most complex string of faulty thinking into short, sweet chains of reasoning that produce understanding. She knows the words that hurt, those that heal, and those that make sense. She took my guilt, my paralytic feelings, and my fears, and made "another person." One that is freer.

High anxiety, which many of my thoughts produce, forbids reason. Reason delivered by bits and bites is how I can push out through the maze and achieve understanding. This process is soothing because it allows me to become grounded in a more manageable framework of reality.

I need instant gratification to remain grounded. It's like eating. I eat words to reach calm. It's my inquisitive mind that has to know the truth that has served me well professionally, but it has put me into hell when I'm in a crisis of confusion.

In her years of counselling, Dr. Edye has formulated some important strategies for containing my mountain of anxiety around the subjects of gender anxiety and sexual identity. I needed information, definitions, understanding, and session after session when I asked more and more questions. I needed also to know about diagnostics, key words, research, genetic information, pretty much all I could grasp in the field of manic depression. What I learned now forms a new vocabulary that she created to help me quell my conflicts, with some degree of success.

I have less fear and a great feeling of equanimity; I'm comfortable in my own skin. However, that doesn't mean that gender confusion is a dead issue. Social phobia can still grip me, and when it does, gender confusion can rise like a demon from a deep cavern. But then I remind myself: I live in the quiet of the forest, where I'm content to read and write and can avoid demanding social occasions.

No, the baggage will never leave. I cannot put any of this in the pigeonholes in the Clickety Clack boxcar. The issues are still very much alive. But I'm no longer a P.O.W. I'm a new person. And I stand tall.

……

DR. EDYE: Because gender and sexual identity work as a fluid entity, I have chosen to comment on both at the end of Chapter 6.

6 Sexual Identity

For most people gender and sexual identity are twins. One informs the other. But that's not true for me. For forty years I could not say whether I was a man or a woman, so I couldn't decide whether I was a heterosexual or a lesbian. I lived in confusion every day, which vastly increased my feelings of total inadequacy and their companions, overwhelming sadness, anxiety, and anguish.

It began with a boy at the age of twelve. It ended fifty years later with a woman whom I love. Was I an accident of birth? Am I a man or a woman? Is there fluidity between the two? How could anyone live this way? Could I maintain sanity?

While worrying about these harrowing questions, I had crushes, attractions, and lusts but didn't act on them. My hormones were frenetic. However, I squashed all impulses to act on my need to be a sexual person. Eventually, though, I was intimate with both men and women. I loved just like everyone else.

My strongest pull was to three women. I was sexually intimate with one and had a long-term companionship with the other two. I loved all three deeply, and still do, even though one is gone from my life.

At age twenty, I became attached to a girl, nearly a woman, who was marvellous, witty, and full of adventure and laughter. It was my first love affair. I spent most of my waking hours near her or with her. I was ecstatic. I revelled in the excitement of intimacy; I was in awe at the revelation of loving arms, and being accepted for who I was, with no judgments attached.

When my father discovered the extent of our interest in each other, he offered me $500 not to be "friends" with her. Of course I didn't want to change anything about our relationship; I was crazy about her and I thought she felt the same attachment to me. But it turned out that she had other plans anyway. I had to let her go. She was to be married. I was heartbroken.

When I recovered from that, I eventually began to see a man. He lit up the heavens, for a while anyway, but when the fire of sex diminished, I told him that I had a steady boyfriend and that I didn't want him any more. I jilted him on the excuse that I had met someone overseas. Despite my rather cruel treatment of him, our relationship recovered and we remained each other's best friend for the rest of his life. He was exciting, handsome, strong, all I would have wanted in a man. We managed, rather easily, to keep our intimate relationship at bay after he was married. Oh, I was jealous, and it was hard sometimes. I can tell you this: One day, walking down Portage Avenue, Winnipeg's main street, holding hands, he stopped and took my hand. He said to me, "I should have married you." My heart sang, even after thirty years of knowing him.

Apart from these relationships, I, mostly, had barren times. I knew men were not attracted to me sexually. It hurt, but I understood. Like an animal, I gave off signals that I was off limits. And it's just as well, because I couldn't have endured a sexual encounter. I tried, now and then, always with terrible regrets afterwards about being a non-performer. I could not afford to fail again and again. So I refused invitations. My father's voice was always present: "Don't you ever shame this family."

While men were not attracted to me socially or sexually, I could always count on some attention for the conversation I could initiate. I was interested, passionately, in sports, business, finance, and politics, and in fact, was fully engaged in the latter. At a cocktail party, I would gravitate toward any group of men talking on these subjects while rejecting totally groups of women talking about diapers and babies.

In my forties and fifties, my body still ached for the warmth of another, as it did in my twenties. The loneliness was suffocating. I knew my life was bound up in guilt. I felt it was a tragedy. I needed to find refuge, and I went looking for it. What else was there to do?

During that time, I engaged in two encounters that still cause me remorse because they were hurtful to the other person. It is difficult to think of these, but I try to forgive myself, knowing the enormous pain I was struggling with.

Maybe some people knew of my depression at the time; certainly most distanced themselves from me. Perhaps they thought of me as a "queer" and were afraid of being tainted, or maybe I was judged to be too mannish. Whatever the case, I was judged negatively for trying to find a few minutes of solace in enfolding arms. I know one thing: I was never asked for a date again.

You'd be surprised at how a knowing hug can bring the restoration of energy and faith to a kindred soul. I remember my psychiatrist saying, "You know, there will come a time when sex and intimacy won't be as important." He was right about the sex, but oh so wrong about intimacy. We all need touch, simple stroking and the sense that we are with someone who matters to us. My long-time relationships have been asexual.

My second "love" happened at age forty-five with a young woman of thirty. Dawn seemed to adore me. For ten years, our life together was enormously exciting. We travelled widely for business and pleasure. With a creative artist, we formed a public relations and advertising agency which was highly successful. We did a work stint for the Government of Canada in the Caribbean; we worked overseas and throughout the United States. Later, we began a long-term project of producing audiotapes for cancer patients and their families.

Together we grew personally and professionally. However, in the eleventh year, she felt "stirrings" of her own. It was time to reach out and be with men. Soon I had to ask her to leave; I was heartbroken and had turned jealous, suspicious, and angry. I was on my way to utter madness.

My third relationship is with Joey, whom I have known for fifty-five years. She is seventy-four, twice married, and I am sixty-nine, never married. We are two peas in a pod, committed to one another for the rest of our lives, supportive and sharing in every way, but without sexual involvement. We enjoy the support of our friends and her family, and feel safe and secure together. Truly, Joey is the love of my life, if you define love in its term of pure caring and openness (no secrets). With Joey, my mental health has improved, and finally I feel free.

Joey's support and encouragement have helped me learn how to internalize my sexuality, and yes, I have not only defined it, but I live with that knowledge now in a settled way. That is not to say I don't have difficulties in my thinking, but I can go back to an equation to remind myself that I am not a transsexual (a great fear); I am forty percent woman and sixty percent man. My "maleness" makes me attracted to women because my brain takes me in that direction. Of course, it's all a moot point now that I'm sixty-nine.

......

You could ask me about "externalizing" my gender identity to match my sexuality. As I have said, I prefer mannish clothes, even though I have always dressed appropriately for social and business occasions. However, now that I'm retired, I can wear my housecoat all day!

Adding to what I said in the last chapter about clothes, there was a time when I could not go through a department store without being drawn to the men's department. If I was with my good friend Elaine, or I was alone, I could shop to my heart's content. But, if I was with someone who didn't know my bent, I'd have to leave the department sad and unfulfilled.

When I was feeling very confused about wardrobe issues in the early seventies, my GP commented one day on my large watch and gold signet ring: "Too big, too mannish."

"No," I said. I explained that I valued these items that I had bought rather than the feminine ring and watch my father had given me.

On another occasion, the same GP told me that I needed some lessons in the art of femininity. For the next five days, I was to come to his office at the lunch hour dressed "to the nines," looking "well turned out." If I didn't follow through on this series of "classes," I knew that he'd tell my father.

So I teetered in each day in high heels, a dress, or a skirt and jacket, with earrings and feminine jewellery, looking like the perfect Miss Dress-Up. He'd sit behind his desk and look me up and down. If I didn't pass muster, I had to endure critical comments. It was a terrible week, after which I was furious, with nowhere to take my anger. Imagine the gall of both men!

There were other problems with that GP. I am still embarrassed for him. He understood nothing about issues relating to gender and identity. Once, while giving me an annual check-up, he brushed against my breast and then asked, "Are you aroused?" I was repulsed, but I cushioned the blow. Instead of yelling, I said, "I feel nothing. You are too old for me!"

He often asked if there was a "problem" with my sexuality, and I once said, "I'm probably a latent homosexual. Is that a 'problem' for you?" Then I went to a women's clinic across the street and finally got myself a new doctor.

In "cases" like mine, I believe the work around identity is a personal one. It requires separation of one identity (gender) from the other (sexuality). When the gender issue is resolved, the issue of sexuality will also be resolved. As well, I believe that there isn't a necessary connection between mental health problems and sexuality, unless it raises its ugly head beyond the scope of heterosexuality.

In my case, I spent most of my life living under a cloud of judgments, ones that I could have erased if I'd had the counselling and appropriate support. For roughly thirty-five years, I got nowhere trying to answer my question about sexuality. I lived in a vacuum so that I could ease my anxiety and continue to function.

When I started to work with Dr. Edye, all the confusion was resolved over several conversations. A solution finally emerged! "If I am more man than woman, then sexually, I must be more man than woman." This explained my attraction to women and led me to understand that I'm heterosexual, not homosexual. In the space of a year, I had both a gender and a sexual identity. Wow!

This "wow" does not mean I can put sexuality into a Clickety Clack pigeonhole. There are still moments of angst, but Joey and Dr. Edye bring voices of reason into my life.

I am leaps and bounds ahead of where I was, stuck for forty years in a world where I had no identity.

……

DR. EDYE: Let me explain the terms "gender identity" and "sexual identity." Gender identity refers to whether a person thinks of himself or herself as a woman (feminine) or a man (masculine). Sexual identity refers to whether a person is sexually or romantically attracted to men or women.

So, physical identity (male/female), gender identity (masculine/feminine) and sexual identity (lesbian, gay, bisexual, heterosexual) can exist in any combination.

In current psychiatric terminology, gender identity disorder is diagnosed only if someone experiences persistent discomfort with his or her gender role, as well as an intensive and persistent tendency to manifest stereotypical behaviour of the opposite gender such as sexual fantasies and cross-dressing.

Not so long ago, homosexuality was treated as a mental illness but is no longer. It is now recognized, socially and medically, that non-heterosexuality is not deviant or even unusual.

Jung, an early psychoanalyst, believed that everyone has male and female aspects and that awareness of both was necessary for mental health and personal growth.

Joy and I have talked at length about her gender identity and sexual identity. I have told her that gender identity and sexual identity are both on a continuum. She doesn't need to have a label nor would I find it appropriate or accurate. She simply "is."

Joy sees herself as a forty/sixty, that is, forty percent female and sixty percent male. It is not surprising that Joy was often paralyzed by the fear of discovery in a society that was largely unsupportive and judgmental. Joy has wondered whether her identity issues are a result of her mental health problems and even wondered whether she has multiple personalities. I don't see evidence of this.

Sadly, Joy describes a boundary violation by a trusted physician, when he claims to test her sexual orientation by brushing her breasts. Notwithstanding the belief at that time that homosexuality was a mental illness, his actions were a violation of Joy's body and mind.

Joy's drive to integrate gender and sexual identities has been a life-long mission undertaken with great fears but fuelled by purpose and courage. As she struggled and accomplished her goals, she became more settled and "self" confident. As a result, she can now express other facets of her creativity with conviction and freedom.

7 Electroconvulsive Therapy

Electroconvulsive therapy. ECT. Electroshock therapy. In the 1950s and 1960s, it was given to clinically depressed patients who did not respond to medication. I was a perfect candidate for this mind-numbing procedure because, like many people with a profound depression, I didn't respond to the inadequate drug therapies of the time. I was also a prime candidate because electroconvulsive therapy was sometimes delivered to the "sexually deviant" as aversion therapy. It was promised that the therapy would cure my (supposed) homosexuality, as well as my depression. It did neither.

My journey towards electroshock therapy began with drug therapy for severe depression in the fall of 1960, several years after my diagnosis as a manic depressive. I had been a guinea pig for several medications, some with strict diet restrictions. Each new drug had nasty side effects: vomiting, mouth sores, "iffy" gut, weight loss, heavy head, violent headaches, and more. None of these drugs did any good.

My depressive symptoms continued unabated (as did

my hypomania, a forerunner of mania.) Strangely, I didn't know that I was extremely sick. The label "manic depression" had not been used in my presence. It was another black mark against me that my father tried to stomp out.

My mother's younger sister had manic depression and her father before her had also had it. She was hospitalized to undergo electroconvulsive therapy treatments in some of the same years as me. What I experienced at home were only the whispered voices of my parents. I often think they might have felt cursed that this illness had popped up in three generations on my mother's side of the family. And that was why it was hidden. The closet was filling up with another horrible secret.

Despite this history and my treatments, my parents were determined that I be seen as normal. So, when I graduated from university, despite the risks, they allowed me to take the obligatory trip to Europe to see the sights, while contemplating post-graduate studies.

I had companions on the trip. We were to have picked up a car in Germany. However, one of the girls noticed I was acting "funny," phoned her parents and mine, and several hours later I was on a plane to London.

So my traditional year overseas after graduation was shortened. I was sent to see a psychiatrist in London who, because of symptoms he recognized in me—though he did not share his diagnosis with me—insisted that I return home right away. He gave me some pills and I flew home immediately.

Shortly after my arrival home, my father, without my consent, had me committed to undergo a battery of electroconvulsive therapy treatments. He was determined to have me "fixed." I was not "offered" the treatment. It was done without consent. This treatment was not ever discussed by my parents with me. What he did is make a bargain on my behalf with the devil, and I never knew the details for many years, until quite recently.

For me, ECT was the thief of memories and self-worth. A brain fry. Stupefying. And it was administered without my consent some thirty times between 1960 and 1963. The perpetrator of those stolen years: my father. To the end of her life, my mother continued to refer to these treatments using euphemisms, and on her dying bed, she asked me to "forgive your father." I cannot forget and I cannot forgive. As I recollect…

In the waiting room I sit in terror. I wear an ugly blue gown, a hideous striped, blue dressing gown that covers only parts of my body. New slippers, though. Who gave me those? I feel as if I'm on my way to the executioner but no hood to hide behind. My body stinks of the familiar nervous sweat that I used to love in locker room days. People dressed like me are waiting for the same event, the only thing we have in common.

I do not look—and neither do they. We are soldiers in a camp, each person selfishly protecting his small space of being: a very old and torn vinyl chair. I sneak a peek. Across the room, I see an older lady. As I look around, I notice that everyone is older than I am; and there are more women than men. All keep their heads bowed. Me too. I am ashamed. I hate being here. I am a prisoner. I am so scared. My heart races. I can't hold my knees together in a lady-like way, as I was taught. Who cares? This is definitely not a tea party! I was not invited here; I did not come willingly. I am a captive in a locked ward, who trudged down to the bowels of this freaky, cold hospital in lock step with the others, shepherded by a nurse who had a silly old-style white cap on her head—and a man in white—but he didn't look like Mr. Glad. He looked big, strong, and he kept us marching.

I follow the others who also look glassy-eyed and terrified. I don't belong here, I scream inside. What did I do? Why am I here? I don't know what is to happen to me... I haven't been told one damn thing. How long will I be in that room across the hall, or what happens after, or worse yet, where will I be taken? I didn't say "yes." No one is here to protect and love me, to be with me. I am so afraid. I don't understand why anyone would make me do this.

My name is called. Obediently, I rise to follow the nurse. My head starts to spin. I try not to look as I enter the room. I don't want to see the equipment. I call it the black box, when, in fact, it was brown (but I always call it black, because it is dark—and evil).

I see the big, bushy, uneven eyebrows of Dr. A.—and his very dark brown, beady eyes. I feel sick to my tummy, and I feel like I am either peeing or pooping myself. I don't care... I see the eyes of his son, his assistant, who is only seven years older than I am. This is embarrassing—even in my heightened state ... I climb on the table. People take hold of me. I can smell the room. I know there is anesthetic coming, and I hate the mask. I've had surgery before, so I know the smell. I hate white, especially men in white coats—doctors—nurses, too, for that matter.

White means pain ... I am told to do "this and that." My pulses races ... The jelly that goes on my temples messes my hair. I feel the needle prick the skin; I taste the sodium pentothal ... then comes a weird shudder inside my head. I go to oblivion, leaving, sinking, surrendering the care of my brain, myself, to strangers around me, people I do not know, do not trust.

I cannot tell you what they did to me—I only know what I have learned in dribs and drabs much later in life. (Funny, I was never curious enough to ask.) I know that bilateral electrodes were placed on top of the temple jelly and someone got to flip a switch (or whatever) and my self-worth and early years (zero to twelve, approximately) were gone, stolen in a flash of electricity, a grand mal seizure. The first thing I remember in that recovery room was the taste of cotton batten.

I did not recover. I survived! No taste. No saliva. A metallic mouth. Nice nurse. Achy legs, neck. Weak. I had a froggy voice, so I couldn't even talk to myself. Soft words. Blotto. Sometimes I'd wake up in my bed near the window, my only link to the outside. I went to occupational therapy in a dungeon, where all these people, fried like me, were doing silly things. I was to knit! Ha! I started, the afghan grew and grew, from what was to be a scarf into a jagged rug, and from there to the junk heap, I guess.

Unending trooping to the ECT room. Feelings of horror. I am a zombie. I have done so many bad things. More treatments, more waiting for someone to come and say, "there, there dear, it'll be over soon. You are a good girl." But no one did. The nights were dark—shadows on the walls, people with big rings of jangly keys. I never went anywhere. Just Bed Two on the Psycho Ward. Locked in, no one to talk to. Brusque nurses. Did I eat? I don't remember, except for medications, apple juice (I hate it to this day!) and Coke—never drank it again.

And then one day my father came and took me home. Where was my mother? I kept looking out the window... and crying... that's the only feeling I had, but I don't know why I cried. What for? The terrible thing is I had to go back to that room. I "graduated" to outpatient, and one time I was with my aunt, waiting for the white coats in that room. Who took me home after? Did someone pick up my aunt? Or did we go by cab? Who knows? When did it all end? I think the spring of 1963.*

ECT is an abbreviation for what the public knows as shock therapy. As I later learned, the first delivery of ECT as an electrically-induced seizure was to a thirty-nine-year-old man suffering from manic and psychotic episode in a Rome hospital. The date was April 11, 1938.

In various forms, ECT was used until it fell into great disfavour after the Second World War. There was an enormous backlash and worldwide public outcry due to the many atrocities performed during the Nazi era on mentally ill patients. ECT re-emerged in the 1950s, and then fell into

*This account comprises excerpts from an article written by the author and edited by Jeffrey L. Geller, MD, MPH, for use in *Psychiatric Services: A Journal of the American Psychiatric Association*, Vol. 56, January 2005, pp. 34–5.

another period of damnation, mostly because of issues of abuse, personal rights, and lack of patient consent. It was reborn when psychotropic drugs, developed in the 1960s, failed to help patients whose depressive illnesses turned out to be drug-resistant. After 1978, many controls for ECT were legislated to produce a process of patient consent, a process re-evaluated over the years under the various lobbies of patient advocates to what it is today.

There is danger in writing about this subject for me. It conjures up too many emotions: fear (still), bubbling anger, burning resentment at yet another "secret" that had to be hidden, and sadness at what my life might have been without ECT. It changed the direction of my life, forever.

The beginning of my ECT treatments also marked the beginning of what I refer to as my stolen years: a ten-year gap (1960 to 1970) during which time I had three years of ECT followed by seven years of recovery, rediscovery, and thought about "what to do" next.

This was the decade when I was young, frightened, fragmented. I did not know what was going on with me, or my mind. This was also the time during which my friends fell in love, married, had babies, went to graduate school. I, however, sat in a room (either in hospital or out) staring through a window at nothing, just a blank slate for a life. You could say, "Oh! She's feeling sorry for herself." And you'd be right. However, I think that while a dash of self-pity may be somewhat self-indulgent, it is also normal, and can be a fine motivator to get one off one's butt. It was certainly accurate to say that much passed by me in those years, never to be experienced, recaptured, or more importantly, understood—until now.

The nature of the treatments, not to mention the sheer

number of treatments, was an invasion of the core of my being. And never did I say, "You have my permission to do *this* to me." I was a victim of ECT. ECT was barbaric abuse. No amount of research and reading has ever persuaded me otherwise.

Yet, it was all there was to "help." I know that, and because I accept that, those times are rarely in my thoughts. Plumbing my memory for details has been both tough and cathartic.

As for my parents, "They knew not what they did." Giving their behaviour a biblical spin has been my way of putting the experience to bed. After the treatments, they wanted ECT banished from their vocabulary. They made it disappear by denying that it had happened. They were gripped by fear. Fear was everywhere. I could see it, taste it, smell it, and it appalled me, always. And they responded to their fear by acting: they put me out of sight. I never did forgive my father, however, for signing the consent without telling me (asking me?!) something, anything. Where were the explanations to help with my fear?

The experience of ECT is as clear to me right now, and pardon the pun, electrifying, as when I had my first treatment in the dark winter of 1960. ECT and the memory of it is a rough frame frozen in its time. It left a searing imprint on my brain. Dehumanizing. The smells and disorientation are horrifying. My brains were scrambled. And, incredibly, a procedure to help "cure" my ills broke my spirit completely.

As a result of ECT, my early years have been lost to me. My memories of childhood come from one scrapbook that shows my mother's early life, and a glimpse of mine—a dozen photos. My earliest memories, insofar as they exist, were implanted by my grandmother and aunt. They are not real. I have great difficulty going to school reunions. It's chilling not to remember faces or experiences, though I try.

As a means of dealing with the anxiety that this gap in my memory induces, I developed a coping strategy: I retreated to a "place" where all was "perfect." Sometimes these places were imagined; sometimes they were half-imagined. I treated my friends' homes as my own, and their parents as my surrogates. I also learned how to create a make-believe world where all is "perfect." Often, though, I simply retreated to the place in the world where I felt safest: Victoria Beach, where I would come in the summertime with my grandmother. There were no people there, no angst; it was silent except for the sound of the waves. There was only water, blue sky, and hot sun on the soft sand. To this day I use this image to calm myself.

In addition to memory loss, another problem with ECT, one which is rarely mentioned, is that it breeds and feeds narcissism. One cannot help but focus on the self, and yet the real job is to turn that focus elsewhere. But who teaches the "tricks of the trade" that can assist recovery and motivate someone to create a new life? Recovery is a revolting merry-go-round of learning, re-learning, re-adjusting, dealing with ECT memory gaps, re-engaging with life and friends, but keeping your "secret." And the secret doesn't go away; it stayed with me along with all my scary thoughts. I owned them, alone, for forty-five years—until now!

I still have doubts that there are adequate descriptions given of the treatment process and side effects. I implore healthcare professionals to fully explain to prospective patients the procedure, the feelings, the emotions, and the attempt at recovery of memory, so that they and their family members will experience fewer life-changing "surprises." This can help prevent someone else losing so much of herself, which was my experience.

Closed doors. Jangly keys. Rattle, rattle. I'm locked in on myself. I need to get free. Breathe, deeply. The feeling will pass. I will always suffer from the need to flee. But, I wasn't going to join my friend who took her life with anti-depressants and Scotch. I decided to just get the hell out of that house! Finally, a goal: GET OUT! I did... I began to take risks. I began to live, and shortly after being released from the hospital, I bloody well did get out of that house that was never a home. I got a place of my own. A studio apartment that I decorated with old furniture, tables, linens, and pots and pans from my grandmother's basement. Then Life began to happen, slowly and more deliberately.

There would be heydays to come, but I needed to shed all vestiges of the mantle of ECT. In the years after my ECT, I did pull myself up by my bootstraps. I grabbed some grit, left Dr. A. and psychiatry behind. It was a brave new world for me. I got into graduate school at the University of British Columbia on a scholarship, specialized in mass communication, got a career as a librarian, and then switched directions because I had a passion for writing. I craved the freedom of the late sixties—a life without rules.

In that period I resented that I had to invent creative ways to hide the lost years: I had to say I was out of town, travelling, studying, whatever, in order to satisfy an application for graduate school or a job. Lies, lies, lies.

By the way, it wasn't until I saw *One Flew Over the Cuckoo's Nest,* many, many years later—I took a friend to emotionally hold onto—that I had any hint of what electroshock looked like. Not that this movie was accurate in its depiction of ECT, but I had never thought to ask about the procedure until this moment. I was in disbelief. It was barbaric. That same evening, I felt exactly as I did after my ECT: dirty, stigmatized and isolated. I knew then that I was set apart; I came from another planet.

Although my life was massively altered by ECT, it has been sad, wonderful, fragile at times, fearful at others, but always filled with work, travel, great colleagues, a few close friends, and now Joey, who cherishes my otherness as normal. Life does make a circle, if you let it.

......

In spite of five rounds (each round is six to twelve treatments) of ECT and a lot of drug therapy in the 1970s, when new psychotropic drugs became available, my times could be characterized in one phrase: some good days, some bad, but "it was all that could be done."

At public seminars and conferences, I am often asked whether I would consider having another "run in" with ECT. I have thought long and hard about it, and can answer it by addressing the three questions that tend to emerge in these settings: Are medications really necessary? If medications fail, should ECT be considered as an option? Would I consent to ECT, if all other treatment failed?

Medications: I understand, clearly, why some people do not take the medications prescribed for a major mental illness. No one enjoys the side effects. Medications are integral to my daily functioning. They are part of my toolkit, forever. Breakdowns are unacceptable to me, so I have never been off my regimen of the day.

ECT treatment as an option: My readings tell me that antidepressants are effective in only fifty percent of treatments of extreme cases of depression. ECT is effective in seventy-five to ninety percent that are urgent in nature. That makes ECT an important option for patients who can make a fully educated decision.

There is a burgeoning interest in the use of electroconvulsive therapy, particularly for people who do not respond to drug treatment. It can help a person escape from a living hell. I have read that ECT is the treatment of choice for the elderly patient presenting with a depressive component to Alzheimer's disease or dementia. It can dislodge depression and mania more quickly than drugs, since drug regimens frequently require a trial of different antidepressants, something which can take considerable time, in order to find one that will prove effective.

For myself, I do worry that, at some point, as the literature says, my bipolar drugs will lose their efficacy and I will be less responsive. There is a risk that some antidepressants can accelerate cycling of bipolar disorder. This makes ECT for severe bipolar depression more reasonable to consider.

There have been some bitter battles over the use of ECT. And I have heard countless stories over the years. Aside from supporting ECT as a possibility for treatment, I add this comment: We are people. We must judge what is right for ourselves, with the information and guidance of others. I come at the subject of ECT from a different time; today the healthcare system is much different. We must measure our choices now by the progress that has been made to save us from pitfalls of the past. Who are we who had ECT in the old days to judge what is right for you now? You must be an educated patient.

For better, for worse, I have a view of ECT coloured, obviously, by my very own set of circumstances. ECT may not have served me well, but it gave me several years of "reprieve" from severe symptoms.

Would I submit to ECT now if drug therapy failed me? Since I began working on this book, I have begun taking lithium medication, and it is working wonders. I have also recently learned that I would not be a good candidate for ECT again. So, it looks like I will never have to face that question. However, if I had to submit in order to get another chance to go on living, then I would need a mittful of information to fully understand ECT as it has progressed.

......

There's a postscript to my incarceration on the psych ward, which rings true for those of us who have been committed. It was written by Sara Johnson in 1949. She was a patient at the Brandon Mental Health Centre in Manitoba. Her poem was found in the archives of that institution, which also holds the names of many inmates who were buried in unmarked graves, because family members did not collect their bodies after death. The poem is entitled "Ode to a Key."

Rattle, rattle little key
How I hate the sight of thee
Only thou can open the lock
Of the door at which I knock
From early morning to late at night
Oh, how wretched is my plight
Each locked door at which I stand
Will only open at thy command
When carried by a nurse's hand
Thou art like a fairy's wand

Strongest lock gives way to thee
Oh, thou powerful little key
When filled with anger or with woe
I to a quiet spot would go
There to sit alone and sigh
Or mop the teardrops from my eye
I find as oft I've found before
That thou has once more locked my door
Doesn't thou wonder little key
That I hate the sight of thee
The world is ruled so someone said
By the hand that rocks the crib
But the hand that holds the key
Rules the globe it seems to me.

How can I tell you the relief that came to me as I joined my imaginary friends aboard the Clickety Clack train? I could not go often, because I had no brain to imagine anything. But, when I was able, I did. Usually, I was in a quiet mood. Oddly enough, I sensed that, because my own "train" was out of control during my treatment time and recovery, I had to stay clear of imagination, which I had always used for comfort.

When I was able to go more frequently, Mr. McIntosh and Ernie had their ears talked off over those ten years. I was embarrassed to have been institutionalized. But these men helped me to understand that none of these events had been in my control. I also learned that I wasn't bad; people had been bad to me.

Also, I discovered that I could trust, but only if someone could talk to me about an uncomfortable subject, so I could see his or her "stripes." I had trouble with cognition in the immediate post-treatment period but the boys would give me exercises to start remembering names, faces, experiences, the lot. We three dipped into all the terrible things that had happened in the ECT room, and the emotions that tickled the surface of my mind day and night. They were my voices in the night when I was alone and fearful. Their conversations ran through my head to keep me sane. I am grateful for those "friends," and to my rich imagination, to which I have returned time and again. It has rarely failed me.

......

DR. EDYE: Joy describes two of the reasons that led her father to commit her to a hospital and sign forms for her to receive ECT. One reason was her sexual identity. A prevalent belief at that time was that homosexuality could be "cured" by noxious aversion therapy. The goal was to train the brain to have "normal" socially acceptable desires. For those who were unlucky enough to be treated in that era, it is highly unlikely that this goal was accomplished. For Joy, it served only to give her shameful experiences. She was physically removed from society for three years when she otherwise would have furthered her education, begun a career, embarked on relationships, and had the potential to be footloose and fancy-free. She returned home from England in a precarious mental state and her life soon tumbled down. Medications were just beginning to be developed and side effects were generally much more severe than they are now.

Joy's inability to respond to the medications was the second reason for her hospitalization and subsequent treatment with ECT. Its purpose is evidenced by its name: to erase memories both painful and pleasant; to cause such chemical upheaval in the brain that a person could have a "fresh start" in life. The cost of that included confusion, fear, shame, and blunting of the person's ability to process information and solve problems.

Over time, Joy's mental health improved and it is impossible to say why that happened. It could have been the passage of time, as most episodes of depression will resolve over time. ECT may have done something to lift her depression.

In any event, Joy became determined to leave her parents' home and become more independent. She was able to use her keen intellect, determination, and even stubbornness to achieve her goal.

This chapter also illustrates that as the medical profession's knowledge improves, treatments change. Some treatments also change in response to societal pressures. ECT has fallen in and out of favour over the years. It still remains a viable treatment option when a person does not respond to medications or when a person is so acutely ill (not eating or drinking, for example) that without rapid intervention, his or her life is endangered.

Joy and I have talked about whether I would ever recommend ECT for her. It is possible that a medication will fail and that she would then require more intensive treatment. If that was to occur, I have promised her that before considering ECT, we would adequately discuss treatment options, I would also discuss treatment options with her companion or proxy, and all other treatment options would have to first be exhausted.

8 Empty Mirror

"Mirror, mirror on the wall, who's the fairest of them all?" Fleetingly, it shows two images. Neither one looks fair. The mirror is confused.

For many years, I have been told that I have a Jewish soul. I learned the traditions from a family who lived below us in the duplex on Grosvenor Avenue. Many of the traditions ring true to my sense of spirituality, but most of all the tradition of sitting Shiva, a seven-day mourning period for a person who has died. During the sitting of Shiva, people come to the family home to comfort and console, to remember and rejoice. One observance during this time is to drape black cloth over each mirror in the house, to honour the dead one's soul by taking the focus away from oneself.

I believe that my ECT put a cover over the mirror I used in each place I lived. I was in mourning for my soul. I didn't pay any attention to the image, or images, created in my mirrors. I suspect that this could be called a denial of ego—but maybe not, since my ego had been crushed by ECT.

For these "stolen years" after my ECT, I was nobody, and what came to my mirror was an empty shell. I saw it in my eyes. More disturbing than seeing nothing, sometimes I saw two images: what I thought I should see and what I did see.

The urge was always to escape the mirror because it forced me to confront the mammoth job of reconstructing a life. One foot in front of the other. One thought at a time. One task at a time—updating wallet cards, reconnecting with friends, trying to decide who I should be, reestablishing an identity in the world. The list was daunting, but doable, if, and only if, I didn't panic at the magnitude of my undertaking.

What I had to do was put together a full-scale battle plan—no mean feat. Just ask a general. I was doing my own version of a D-Day (Development Day) landing with months of preparation and rehearsals. My basic artillery to cover every flank was comprised of discipline, routine, and journaling, the latter to record and measure progress, reinforce success, and create a strategy for the following day. The major objective each month was to fill a larger fragment of the mirror with one person, in appropriate clothes for a workday, rather than a jumble of two merged images, with different wardrobe requirements.

Let me explain. Every morning before I woke up, my brain had decided who I was. One day, one person; the next day, another. So, each day I had to establish my identity by experimenting with clothes, makeup, and hairstyles. Not until I was fully awake, sitting on the edge of the bed, did

I have an inkling of what direction I would go in—to the "male" cupboard, or the "conservative female" cupboard. Every morning, the same crisis—a pill to quell the attack, then the task of creating a life to present to my public.

I pursued the task methodically, following a course of action that would jibe with the mood and choices presented to me. Start with early morning ablutions, fix breakfast, watch TV to distract myself from the anxiety, take a shower, use the potty (and don't panic if I'm gripped by "the penis conundrum"—the desire to pee like a man, standing up and facing forward), follow the lead to the right cupboard, get dressed, don't look in the mirror, put on lipstick and comb my wavy hair, without really looking in the mirror. If there was some degree of comfort with today's persona, I would march forward into the day. If not, I would return to confusions and panic and the possibility that I couldn't get the day going.

In these days of absolute terror I did not have a psychiatrist, nor do I think one would have been helpful. My first psychiatrist had been unable to relate to young people, and I believed, in my innocence, that I could govern my own path because I had grit and some kind of innate faith that I would be able to decide each day who I was, and then act and dress appropriately. As well, I had the support of "the boys" on the Clickety Clack Bipolar Express. I would fly there in the night to try on various outfits. This practice run allowed me to choose only those outfits that suited me. This helped in the morning because I was able to get up and face the challenge of the day.

The Project of Restoring Joy began early in 1963, three years after the beginning of my ECT—too early as I found out. I was not wholly well, but I was strong in spirit, and determined as hell that I could make a life for myself despite the demons. Surely angels would come to help, I thought.

My parents were normally away for the winter so I took advantage of the time to concentrate fully on my mission. I also took on large "assignments."

When I completed my last round of ECT I weighed ninety-eight pounds, down from 120. I needed new clothes for each cupboard. The female stock came from a shop I knew well, from a salesperson who was excellent; so that was easy. What was considerably harder was visiting the men's wear section of my favourite department store. Here I would ask for a clerk and tell them I was shopping for my cousin. Soon I had the jeans, cords, belts, T-shirts, shorts, and so on, for evenings and the "male" weekends.

I never tried on any clothes in stores. The bags of clothing came home. Then I had to climb the next mountain: Try them on while looking in a mirror.

On went every piece of clothing. Outfit after assembled outfit, traipsing to the bedroom mirror in between—oh, dear! What oomph that took out of me. If I looked acceptable from head to toe, then it was a go. And into the proper cupboard the clothes would go, each set a complete outfit.

Next, with a gift from my grandmother, I bought an MGB roadster. Ooh la la! That picked my spirits up by leaps and bounds. Soon I was out roaming the streets, but always close by in the neighbourhood. Racing while being secure. Silly. But I had my ways of creating a comfort zone.

I became a fan of two more routines. On Friday nights, I went to the movies, cozied up with a big bag of buttered popcorn, and tried out my casual "female" clothes to see if I blended in with a crowd. Early on Saturday morning I would put on my real leisure clothes and cowboy boots, go to Salisbury House, and sit at the counter with the truckers. I had pancakes and bacon with half a jug of syrup and the morning newspaper for company. Just a regular guy.

Practice. Practice. Makes perfect? No! But it made things less imperfect and easier. Month after month I began to fill the bathroom mirror with more fragments of my image.

I became cocky. I got a position at the Winnipeg Public Library as a clerk. The strain was enormous. Dressing every day, putting on a bold face. I wanted this job to work. I also needed the money. Moreover, I needed the reinforcement of living up to my well-thought-out plan.

Even though the plan needed more time to bring results, I did this job well, which earned me a scholarship to the University of British Columbia's Library and Communications program. I thought being a bookworm again was a job I could handle. I shipped my car out by train, which became a funny story. Since my father was in the sugar business, he arranged to put my MG sports car inside a rail car which was destined for Vancouver. When I went to find it at the warehouse, it was sitting covered in sugar with only its hood showing. The rest of the story isn't so funny, though. I only lasted one semester and returned home feeling I was a failure.

It was time to re-evaluate the plan. ECT had stolen more than memories. It had stolen my self-confidence and my chutzpah. What seemed necessary after the failure at UBC was to go slowly into the workforce. I began to read every section of the newspaper again so that I'd be "current" when talking to people, not some dummy vacuum brain. I also paid a great deal of attention to the want ads—not the executive jobs, but the part-time work, because I thought I'd be more likely to succeed at something less demanding.

Dates, months, and some events are occasionally murky in these years. However, I continued to concentrate on the plan. It was the only way I would get stronger. I learned patience. I knew I'd get there, wherever there was. My life was a wide-open road, and I stayed clear of driving it in one particular direction. I told myself: "Let it happen. Don't judge progress. Don't worry if you take one step forward, and two back." Thanks to another generous gift from my grandmother, I was able to pay for my tuition and finally complete my studies, graduating with a degree in Mass Communications in 1965. I was feeling like I was pretty hot stuff.

In the winters, I had two part-time jobs: first at a farm machinery company where I began a newsletter for farmers and members of various Hutterite colonies. The experience was exciting and the people fascinating. Learning a new culture so foreign to mine was stimulating. The other job was at my uncle's flower shop, where I organized and managed the books. During busy times—Christmas, Easter, Valentine's Day, and Sadie Hawkins (an old custom whereby the girls take the boys out for a date and buy them huge, long corsages with flowers and keepsakes)—I made boxes, trimmed thorns off roses, wrapped mums each with tissue, one dozen to the box. Sometimes, if the shop was very rushed, I would drive the van on delivery.

Every chore associated with these two jobs kept me hoping, thinking, practising my real job of being me. I found appropriate clothes and studied the actions of others so that I would have models for creating my own persona. Even if I had a panic attack, I was learning I could control it by turning my attention to some detail of what I was doing. That worked like a charm. I gained confidence. More importantly, I felt useful.

It was time to take another leap. I answered a help-wanted ad for the position of clerk at a local library. I was over-qualified and lacked experience. The boss was an unkind lady and we clashed. She would gnaw at me to take on more responsibility, and because I was afraid of another failure, I took her challenge and broke under her incessant pressure. She fired me.

I took unemployment benefits, and often whimpered myself to sleep. How was I going to succeed if I couldn't stick to a job? How could I be a fine, upstanding person? How could I stand among my friends and talk of my work as though it were equally valuable?

The following year, 1966, was a fallow time. I was dormant and depressed again. How was I going to lift myself out of the doldrums? I was tired of the plan. And yet, it was exactly what I needed for this unsteady journey back from the wilderness of ECT. I had to understand that I wasn't to blame for my failings. There were explanations; never mind. I finally decided to make a new plan, but one not so detailed or lengthy. I'd take it one step at a time.

Then, in February 1967, I hit the jackpot: a job at A&W International, the chain of hamburger joints that was spreading rapidly from its base in the United States to Canada. Winnipeg was the head office of the Canadian operation, and I got hired as a writer of a monthly magazine and technical manuals such as one for new employees that explained "how to cook a hamburger in five easy steps." The executives were young men, full of vigour, guts, and gumption. They had a plan. I was excited, and within several weeks I knew that I would belong, a new and foreign emotion for me, but one with which I became comfortable. I'd go home at night and pinch myself. Finally, I had a job into which I could throw myself completely; I knew I would succeed.

Soon I rose through the ranks and earned more money. My comfort turned into confidence. I asked for a newly opened position as an advertising writer, and got it. And for the first time, I was introduced to the power of photography. I fell in love. The camera was a mirror through which I could see other images, beyond myself. And, as a friend said recently, the camera never lies. I grew within myself as surely as I grew in capability, energy and creativity. I was successful. I asked for and got new challenges dropped in my lap.

With the encouragement of a man who knew the game of advertising and how to get the most out of me, I started to travel to Chicago, where A&W had contracted a forward-looking ad agency. In this arena, not only was my brain exercised, but I learned the art of people work, presentation skills, as well as more and more about photography—how to use your eye to determine the right image for your product. My advertising "eyes" had great value, I was told. I understood, intuitively, more about images that were productive and smart, that drove home the message.

Another benefit of my trips to Chicago was that I also had the thrill of shopping for myself (that is, my "cousin") in Brooks Brothers, the home of men's classy button-down shirts.

Suddenly, I discovered myself. I saw myself clearly, and every day that I worked led to a better tomorrow. I was on my way—not sure where, but I began to like what I saw. I had started on the road to loving myself and acquiring the skills to survive in a tough industry. I came to peace with the brand of bipolar disorder I suffered at the time (it has changed) and to the ups and downs of the symptoms, at least for a while.

Despite the downs, when I would experience flights of fear and have to get out of the office to breathe, I learned, experimented with styles of writing, became even more passionate about photography, and trained my eye so that I could master the world through the lens.

Time passed quickly, and in 1969 I accepted a senior position with the firm. However, I needed to see more of the world through my own eyes and a camera lens. So I returned to London, but a different person than in 1960. After a good rest at the seaside with my aunt, during which time I survived the noise, the crowds, cocktail chatter, and the ever-present clothing issues, I returned to my job in Winnipeg, refreshed.

I'll never forget that May morning. I was dressing for work, and I turned to look in the mirror. I covered more of the surface than ever before. I liked what I saw. I was saucy to the sight. Miraculous! After six years of executing my plan, I was seeing awesome results. I took a hand mirror from my mother's dresser and looked again. My grandmother would say, "I like the cut of your jib." Or, "You look swish." I did.

The question now was, "What to do?" I had to keep moving; if I stopped, I was afraid that the curtain would come down and I'd be in the dark again.

In May 1970, on a Thursday afternoon, the phone rang in my office; it was the president of the University of Winnipeg. I knew him through family connections and couldn't imagine why he was calling me. He inquired whether I'd be interested in a job at the university. He told me to come to see him on Friday. I told my A&W boss and he encouraged me to take an offer if it was made. "Another step up," he said. I agreed to become the new Director of Public Relations and Publications. A big job. Was I ready for it? By Monday, I was there, hiring staff for a new office.

I was climbing up. However, the mirror was still an uneasy companion. On occasion, I would get frightened at the image. But, inch by inch, I had come to fill the mirror. That, after all, had been the plan.

……

DR. EDYE: Joy begins this chapter feeling dread about looking in the mirror for fear of finding it empty. It ends with her not quite filling the space in the mirror, but delighted to see her own reflection. How did she get there? She developed "The Plan," an exquisitely detailed plan of action. Though she had some ups and downs, some backsliding, she persevered, was amazingly creative, and remained focused on her goals.

She continued to experience anxiety about gender identity, dealing with it in imaginative ways. When living one day as "female" and the next as "male," she was not experiencing multiple personality disorder. Joy's two identities are distinct yet interwoven aspects of her character.

By the end of this chapter, she is performing incredibly well in the workplace, able to meet and surpass all challenges. As I read this chapter, I was thinking that she was rather hypomanic during these days; a little elevated, but functioning extremely well.

9 Heydays

Carpe Diem—Seize the Day!

I was bold, I was brash, I was full of bananas. Nothing could stop me. I had power. I had energy. I had gobs of money. Watch me, world!

In retrospect, it seemed that the mirror had filled toward the end of the sixties, and it had given me a sense of empowerment. I was alive and undaunted. I was thrilled to have a chance to make a fresh start.

From the spring of 1970 to the spring of 1978, I was moving ahead, moving everywhere, doing and seeing, conquering my world, proud of myself, thrilled to be alive, full of life, with no depression, at least none that I gave room to.

Despite my pride at my success in the working world, and my increasing confidence in my own state of mind, I decided to move back "home" in the early 1970s. My mother had been diagnosed with a serious illness and she wanted me there, and I wanted to be with her.

If the truth be known now, I was tickling the edges of

manic behaviour for eight full years. Hypomanic—less than manic—is the correct term. What did I know then about balance? I was simply sailing into horizon after horizon. No one could tell me to stop long enough to smell the roses. I had to keep moving. I was consumed by the need to capture, accomplish, fill my camera with every image of creativity I could. I was me at last. My day in the sun, finally. I burned the candle at both ends. Hang the consequences.

What characterized these eight years were two pastimes: travel and photography, which I pursued with consuming passion. In moving from my condo in 1997, I discovered that I had amassed 137 albums of photos, several dozen from all parts of England, Scotland, Wales, and Ireland. Many were from the Caribbean where, as I have said, I worked for the Government of Canada, but other photos were taken while sight-seeing. I travelled throughout France, Germany and then East Germany, Austria, Switzerland, what was then Yugoslavia, and Poland. I sailed the seas of Greece, Italy, and Spain; took car and train and airplane rides from coast to coast in Canada and the United States.

Much of this travel was done alone, backpacking, at a time when it was quite novel for a woman to be on the road alone. I survived nicely because people were kind and willing to help. I had food and board everywhere I went. All I had to do was ask. Later, I had a year in Israel and six months in Britain on fellowship leave from the university. Heady days!

I must tell you about four albums. In the early days, before I had gained more experience in travel photography, I was fascinated with gravestones, so I had many photos of angels and various other adornments from gravesides.

The second album contained my photos taken at the several Nazi concentration camps I visited in Germany and Poland. Most of the photo slides from these trips I later sold to the CBC for background sources because the work had been done after the Munich massacre when it was difficult to get journalists into some of the areas.

The third album is also precious. The photos come from a long visit to the former Yugoslavia. Then there was nothing but beauty. These slides, too, I sold to the CBC. Many were used in programs describing what was once a beautiful country, most especially along the Dalmatian coast—along which, I might add, I played tennis from village to village, living with locals and taking advantage of invitations to enjoy morning sets on the courts of private clubs.

On one bus trip, I had an uncanny thought about the leader of the tour into communist territory. I felt he might be an agent. At dinner that evening, I approached him and tried to lead him in conversation. Finally he said to me: "Don't ask questions. You could get me in trouble." The encounter revealed how delicate the interactions of people can be and the cover that some men and women had to invent to function in the underground. I thought of this man often when Yugoslavia was torn apart by ethnic conflict.

In the fourth album I have a treasure trove of photographs taken on my two trips to Scotland with my grandmother, Dee. She and I travelled mostly to see her friends and relations. At long last, I met a great-aunt from whom I had received my middle name, Suzanne. We also saw relatives of Dee's husband, Harry, and the sister of my uncle, Mitchell Sharp, one of the other politicians in my family, a great man to whom I became attached as I grew older.

He had been the minister for external affairs in the Trudeau government of the seventies, and though a very busy man, he always had time to fit in a meal with Dee or a coffee with me. We went on to Bexhill, Sussex, England, near Eastbourne, where Dee enjoyed the sea air with Nell, a dear friend, who had become my "aunt." This album of personal photos is very dear to me.

Ten years ago when I moved from my condo, I took many, many hours to sort through all my albums and slides, giving away many pictures to people I felt would find meaning in them. I also held a public sale of photos of all shapes and sizes, photos that had won awards, and photos of outstanding scenery that I had made into postcards, which were really more like works of art. I didn't feel sad about letting so much go. I was proud of the work. What remains is Dee's album and three other albums of my best work, which I continue to admire from time to time.

I travelled far, and wild, taking great pleasure in all aspects of my journeys. I'm happy today that I "front-end loaded" my life. I was in good shape physically. I could hike and walk for miles, and climb mountains. I even climbed down a mountain into a valley to reach a monastery in Yugoslavia, where I was welcomed by the monks and stayed for supper. They gave me a stark room and bed for the night, and a breakfast roll in the morning, before I made my way back up the mountain. I swam in pools made from lava rock, in waterfalls, off a boat, off a canoe. I did what I wanted each day, with nothing standing in the way of getting a photograph.

How did I keep up this pace of travelling? With clear focus and the knowledge that there would come a time when my bipolar illness would not allow me the freedom to travel alone. It was much like a management game: find the target; do the homework; gather the tools together—passport, knapsack, maps, and so on; find an easy mode of transport (motorbike or car); find the energy to be people-oriented; decide what was possible to see; and then go for it! Focus was my main tool.

However, I must be truthful about the exhilaration of my travels. They were filled with periods of mania, which meant that I also had periods of depression. After burning so much adrenalin during a trip, I had to come home for several days of bed rest.

I needed to catch up, to distill experiences into understandable bits for my mind to grasp and enjoy, but most of all I had to adjust to responsibility. I think all this is common for most people. But, for me, I had the added burden of knowing that I was in for a rocky road for a few weeks while I sorted out how to re-enter my world of duality again.

I saw little of my parents when I was home. My father had become an alcoholic, and my mother rode out the booze storms with him without any assistance. I couldn't help her because I had to live my life, and she was fine with that.

However, Mother was deeply hurt and went into a depression when I abruptly left home again. The impetus for my second flight from the house was another fight with my increasingly irrational father. On a "normal" evening, my father had come home begging for one of our many tiffs. I was watching a favourite TV program; he changed the channel. Fireworks started. In a rage, he pulled the TV plug out of the socket, and I left the room and the house, forever. The weekend before, I had rented a small apartment, and had been waiting for an opportunity to tell my mother that I was striking out on my own. That night I took up residence in my new place. Finally, my father was out of my life.

......

A central part of my life during these heydays was my work at the University of Winnipeg. I was a whirlwind of activity. I had no personal life. All my time and energy were devoted to the school. I never felt the need to go beyond the campus, so I saw little of my friends, but kept in touch regularly by phone or postcards. (However, I did join a tennis league. It was therapeutic to smash that ball; some might call it anger management.)

It's hard to describe my job. I was the ultimate Joe Boy. I wrote ads, press releases on visiting dignitaries for media, information on people, articles for magazines, summaries of campus events and happenings, material for fundraising campaigns, and also helped professors polish submissions for scholarly magazines. Over and above that, I acted as assistant to the president, dealing with guest lecturers and performing other public relations duties. I assisted the president and his wife at entertainment functions such as banquets. The years at Government House helped me to command the social aspects of my work, and my years of studying my grandmother McDiarmid were central to my understanding the needs of guests and how best to satisfy them. I was often called upon to speak extemporaneously at gatherings. I helped organize conferences.

I also attended professional conferences in my field inside and outside Canada. I lived and breathed work, and fell into bed at the end of each day so I could be back in my office chair by 8:00 a.m.

All in all, this work at the university brought me immense satisfaction, and also raised my profile. The highlights of these wonderfully crazy years were three special events. The first was a speech given by the former editor of *The Washington Post*, Ben Bradlee, who had managed the paper's attack on Nixon and his henchmen during Watergate. I had the honour of guiding the press conference after Bradlee spoke to a standing-room-only theatre, and later had a cup of coffee and personal visit with him.

Then there was the visit of Simon Wiesenthal, who spoke all over the world to advance his cause of hunting down top-ranked Nazi officials who had escaped punishment after the Holocaust. I took in his press conference as well, which was held under heavy security provided by various government services; their presence was felt throughout the campus, from basements to rooftops. Wiesenthal gave an afternoon address with slide presentation that was absorbing beyond anything I had ever seen. I stood in awe of the man and am certain that my mouth was agape during his talk. Later, I had a chance for a private visit, mostly because I was involved in his evening event, which was an invitation-only fundraiser for his work, attended by members of Winnipeg's Jewish community and various organizations representing Jews in Canada and overseas.

The third highlight was the Commonwealth Congress in 1978, which I attended and had also played a role in organizing. It was made up of 1200 academic delegates from Commonwealth countries gathered together in Vancouver to discuss university and world matters of mutual concern.

Many of these delegates came dressed in the traditional and colourful clothing of their native lands.

A shiver went up my spine when I stepped to the microphone to announce the arrival of dignitaries. As I looked out over the crowd assembled that night, I thought, "What a lucky girl you have been, Joy, to have the opportunities you've had over these years. Where else on earth would this have happened to a person who has the mental troubles I do?"

Four other "happenings" are worth mention:

While at the university, in the mid-seventies, I was encouraged to apply for three different positions at other institutions, two in Winnipeg and one in Seattle. Imagine this: I was short-listed and subsequently chosen as the number one candidate for all three—and on the same day! I was a nervous wreck. What to do? I told the president. I was asked to sit in the anteroom while he got on the phone to the chairman of the university's board and then the chancellor. When he came out he said, "I'd like to buy you a hot dog for lunch!" Off we went to the cafeteria. When we came back, he went into his office, closed the door, and left me sitting in the anteroom again. Suddenly, his office door flew open. He beckoned me inside and referred me to his blackboard. On it, in his chicken scratch writing, were two columns, one for the pros and one for the cons. I read both, and turned to him and said, "OK, I stay." That was it. Nothing more was ever said, and I was at the university for five more years based on requests I had made: that I be responsible only to him, and that my salary be doubled.

Later, with the approval of the president, I took a dive into provincial politics, working as an executive assistant to the Leader of the Opposition, who was a friend. So, I was holding two jobs, which, in hindsight, was foolish. But I thrived on the thrill of the daily skirmishes in the business of politics. In the end, I lasted three years. That was enough; I knew I was running out of gas.

While with the university, I also had the privilege of serving a two-year term as president of the Association of University Information Officers, which allowed me to learn a great deal about the inner workings of every university in the country. Another prime assignment came my way in the mid-seventies, when I was chosen, along with two other journalists, to fly to Churchill Falls, where a mammoth hydro dam was being built. The job: to write on the scale of this undertaking. We stayed in the men's barracks, ate with the guys, got entertained by them, and had a three-day whirlwind tour of the heavy machinery and the vast, beautiful landscape, which allowed us to fully appreciate the scope of the project.

Enough! You get the idea. These were my heydays! The sheer number of events required enormous energy. I used my tried-and-true strategy: "Focus! Concentrate only on what's ahead for the next hour; each hour in the day will take care of itself." Because my general spirit was high, this approach carried the day. But whenever I got worn out, I would take a mental health day. Nobody would ever know what went on behind my apartment door. I lay in bed, trying to close my eyes, and literally let myself spin out of control. People's faces, voices, colours, queer images and thoughts swirled around and around. I'd get up to go potty, have a piece of toast and some tea, and go back to bed again. Generally, if I was free and unafraid of letting my brain take its own course, I was clear-headed the next morning, or at least, as clear-headed as I could be while on medication.

Then I would go another five to six weeks before it was time to hit the "whirly" room again. The plan worked.

Of course, as someone who pretty much lived a lie, I had to constantly guard my tongue. I also had to fiercely control my emotions. Being on "station alert" all the time was enormously tiring. Adding to the burden were my gender and sexuality issues, which were always close to the surface during and after an event. Yet I managed to fake it all and have fun with my dilemma. I could be a marvellous flirt and enjoyed the game; I could also be outspoken and naughty. I was a great dancer, always had been, and knew all the latest moves, although I preferred to lead. I was a star player in those days. Life was shiny and brilliant, until late 1978.

......

DR. EDYE: These were, in many ways, very productive years for Joy. She had tremendous workplace challenges, stimulations, and rewards. True, she had brief crashes, but work was her refuge. Nobody told her to pace herself, to live a more balanced life.

Although Joy doesn't mention it, her diagnosis and surgery for bowel cancer during this period appeared to cause her to flinch only briefly, as she continued to focus on her goals. She met fascinating people, but all the time felt she was living a lie. And life was a pressure cooker: she felt constant pressure to produce more.

10 *Living on the Edge*

My heydays ended abruptly. I felt like the earth and the sky had collided, and I was squished somewhere in between.

During the planning of the Commonwealth Congress in the spring of 1978, my mother's cancer became unbearable for her. A surgical procedure to relieve some pressure in her oral cavity failed and she began to die, in a most horrible way. Her doctor said that "the kindest thing that could happen to Glad is that someone would take her out behind the barn and shoot her in the head. We do that for horses, don't we?"

With help from the marvellous Meta, my mother's housekeeper, and outside help, we managed to keep my mother at home to die, as she had wanted. It was a lonely house. No one came to visit. My father was the gatekeeper and few were allowed in. Mother was his prisoner to the end, as was I. He permitted me just a few visits to say goodbye. The sadness of not being able to talk to her, to tell her things, to have her tell me things still makes me cry, sob, as

I do now as I type. I loved her deeply, even though I didn't know her well.

One request my mother had was "to help your father stay at home to die, and keep him in the style he is accustomed to." I agreed to that. However, I couldn't agree to her second request: "Please, Joy, forgive your father for his treatment of you." I hope she understood why I couldn't. I think she did. He was a manipulative, unfair, uncaring man, who put me through hell. Nothing could make up for that.

Through all this, Dee was also kept from her daughter's bedside. I came from the hospital (where my mother had spent the last hours of her life) on the night of July 17, 1978, to tell my grandmother of Glad's death and weep for losing the mother I never really had.

We buried Glad beside her father a week later, waiting for special friends from other countries to arrive. I had the grave dug double depth.

The sky was dark when I got up the morning of my mother's funeral. I'd had a fitful night and finally needed to write a poem for the service. I had washed my hair, and decided to sit on the balcony to watch the sunrise. An hour or so passed, and as I finished my writing, the sun broke on the horizon. I shall never forget the feeling of absolute calm that came over me. Against a field of blue sky, I knew my mother was watching over me, and expected me to stand tall for the day of mourning and cope successfully with crowds at the reception.

During the service, I held my father's hand often because I could feel his physical and spiritual pain. I know it helped him on the most difficult day of his life. We ended the day in Mother's rose gardens on the bank of the river that went through their property; then I left the house and joined my friends, who were gathered together at another house waiting for me.

......

This seems as good a place as any to give you more of an understanding about bipolar disorder, or in my case, bipolar with psychosis or schizoaffective disorder, as it is now called, because I'm experiencing symptoms as I write this chapter.

I have sobbed for a half-hour now after writing about my mother's death. It isn't so much her death as it is that I could not be with her to help her with the pain of her death; she was alone in a darkened room. Though she couldn't speak, I would have given the world to try and understand what her eyes were saying.

I tried a moment ago to lie down, as I often do in the afternoon to recharge my batteries. I could not lie still. My mind was in a whirling dance. I closed my eyes and saw colours, especially orange, perhaps because there are orange tiger lilies outside my studio window, with the sun playing on their wide tips. I am obsessed. I am beside myself with grief—uncontrollable grief.

She has been dead for nearly thirty years but I still cannot reconcile myself to it. I am obsessed beyond what most people could imagine. But try. Try to think when you are frightened and you can't get rid of the fear. That's obsession. Think of when you close your eyes and you see images. For you, those images are usually temporary. For me, they skid about and twirl until I think I'm going crazy. Well, I am. I am in the midst of mania, right now, despite the fact that

I take a mood stabilizer to prevent extreme mood swings. If I'm not careful, by tonight I'll be at the other end of the spectrum of schizoaffective. I'll be in the pits, in my bed.

The mania right now is painful. My mouth is dry. Then it fills up with fluid; I need to brush my teeth. My heart is racing. My head bangs. My gut scrunches; it feels raw. My hands tremble. I hear noises that bother me; all noise is thunderous, particularly children playing and shrieking. The sheet of my bed is wet with sweat. No one can help me. No one can talk me down. Not even Joey.

What's worse is any word that ends in "–ion" like, say, imagination, becomes "imagina-shun." That's my psychosis picking up on the word "shun," which is the way I feel when people stare at me dressed in "male" ways. I need to ignore the "shun" because I can get stuck in it.

As well, I'm experiencing clanging, or "clickety clack." This is a psychiatric term that refers to one thought quickly becoming another and then another, endlessly.

If all this weren't enough, I also have to deal with my voice. Many people with psychosis hear voices, which you may know from the movies and the way schizophrenics are portrayed in the media. I have only one voice, mine, but it's disassociated from my ego, the seat of my being. As a result, my voice talks to me as though it's a separate entity. Usually it is a protective, intelligent, helpful voice, but several times, as I will tell you later, it has turned on me and instructed me to do things that would harm me. For the most part, I have been strong enough to ignore its commands. On most "healthy" days, I can ignore it, except when I'm writing; then it's most helpful, so I listen.

I also suffer from what is called "cocktail chatter," a term that refers to the sort of background "conversa-shuns" that you would hear at a cocktail party. I can hear the voices but not the words. It's like being hard of hearing and having to turn off your hearing aid to eliminate the indecipherable din. I try to ignore the chatter, but this afternoon, because writing about mother's death makes me too emotional, I am assaulted by most of the symptoms of bipolar with psychosis.

To deal with today's symptoms, I take another management step I have learned through the years: "Stop what you are doing. Get up wherever you are. Walk. Pick up a pen, open your computer, dig in a garden, do anything, then push through the pain." Above all, maintain a focus.

So, today I do something, just enough to allow me to stop the obsession, and with it the grief. That done, in a few hours I should be able to off-load the "exhaust-shun" that comes from the "confu-shun" and return to my writing.

I hope the foregoing account has increased your understanding of some of the symptoms of my illness. If you wish to read about the relationship between mania and creativity, get Kay Redfield Jamison's book, *Touched with Fire*, in which she explains how manic-depression afflicted some of the world's greatest artists.

One more thing. I want to tell you what Rabbi Harold Kushner, author of *Why Bad Things Happen to Good People*, said to me many years after my mother's death. During an interview, he was talking to me about his son who suffered from a rare ailment called progeria, the rapid-aging syndrome. Near the end of our conversation I told him that after my mother had died, I was cleaning out her bedside table and found a small scrapbook I had given her for a Christmas present; it was handmade because I was broke. I had filled it with my poetry and photos of her, my father, my dog, and several of me. I told Rabbi Kushner I had been blocked from being with my mother. He said, "...When she was dying, she was able to summon up memories of you, to look at pictures. You were in that room with her, even if you weren't there physically. She did not die alone..." His words helped me on many occasions to level my grief.

......

Not long after my mother's death, I was told that my fathers' lung cancer had metastasized to his bowel and a tumour was found wrapped around his spinal column. I returned home from a business trip to find him in great pain. I did the best I could, both physically and emotionally. Meta helped and he was able to stay mobile, with a daily display of gumption.

He called me early in the morning after my late night flight the day before. Exhausted, I staggered to the phone and he said: "Get a shower and get over here. We have business to do. No argument. Get a move on." I did. It was close to a thirty-minute drive but I was there before 7:00 a.m.

When I arrived, there was no, "Hello, how are you?" Just, "Sit down, and listen to me carefully." He had his safety deposit box in front of him. Over the next two hours, he went through each paper, explaining what I needed to know, who to call, where to find bank accounts, the whole nine yards. When he was done, I was offered cornflakes and a cup of coffee and told to skedaddle. Nothing on these matters was discussed again, but then there was little time. That was a Saturday in mid-November.

On December 4, in the morning, I had tried to reach

him. No answer. I tried intermittently throughout the morning and into the afternoon without success. Then I phoned my Aunt June, with whom we had enjoyed dinner the night before. He would have called to thank her. She said that he hadn't. I left work, uneasy. I went home, changed my clothes as usual, and then decided I would drive out to the house. As I drove, I became increasingly fidgety. I had a conversation with myself, something like, "If a certain light is on then he's okay; if not, then trouble is waiting in the house."

As I turned the corner of the curved driveway, I saw that the "wrong" light was on. My heart started to race. I had not been given a key for this house so I had no way in. I looked through the back door window. No sign of him in the kitchen, which is where he liked to sit in the morning over coffee with the radio on. I raced over the snowdrifts to the patio doors and hit them with a thud. And there he was, crumpled on the floor. How I ever made it to the front door of the neighbour's (who had a key) I'll never know. I called June and asked her to come to help with the chores that now had to be done.

The neighbour and I entered the house and called my GP. Dad was badly bruised from the fall, so we covered him. The sequence of events thereafter is a blur of activity, but somehow everything got done.

What happened in the midst of all the scurrying was not commonplace and has had a profound effect on me for over thirty years. The GP was the same one that had "teased" me in a sexual way. He took me into the living room and began to grill me in what I thought was an unacceptable way. The questions were all related to what I had done, who I had seen, where I had been since midnight the day before.

Then it struck me: He was trying to find out if I could have harmed my father because I "hated" him. I excused myself ("How dare you leave," he said), went to the phone and called a friend of Dad's who was a lawyer. I asked him to come to the house. Then I went to my mother's room, closed the door, and dared the good doctor to come looking for me. The lawyer arrived and spoke to the doctor but I never learned what transpired between them.

I buried my father on my thirty-eighth birthday, December 7, 1978. We had a birthday party at my apartment afterward. It was a rouser, for young and old. The right thing to do, everyone said.

Ten weeks later I buried my grandmother, my beloved Dee, at the same gravesite.

In the days following, I took a leave from work, and for the first time, I spent some afternoons with Aunt June, who, like me, was now an orphan. Among many necessary topics, we also both talked about the effects of these deaths on our manic-depression conditions. I still treasure this conversation because it gave me a real opportunity to get to know my aunt. Her love and support helped me to get through those difficult times, and I remained very close to her until her death, several years later, from breast cancer.

Despite June's help, however, the death of my parents and, particularly, of my beloved Dee devastated me. I was truly living on the edge. I experienced rolling mounds of grief. I knew about the process; I had studied the steps of grief. But, one can't know until one sits in the middle of the muddle that grief is so overwhelming that it jars the soul.

I went back to work—my salvation. In the evenings, several friends would come with me to my parents' house to help me dismantle it: clothes, personal items, dishes, pots and pans. The house was not something I wanted. It sold overnight. Furniture and other larger possessions went to two weekend sales run by Aunt June. I wanted very few items for myself. It was a wholesale off-loading of possessions that carried too much grief and too many bad memories.

It is said that busy hands keep troubles away. It seemed to work for several weeks. But then I began to have a terrible recurring dream. I was picking up little pieces of my father that were strewn all over the lawn, and putting them in a green garbage bag. That scared me, but I knew, deep down, that the genesis of this nightmare came from the doctor questioning my whereabouts. I also had odd repetitive thoughts. I would drive home from the office and I would find myself whistling. I felt free. I would think: You've got a wad of his money in your purse. Go spend it—on anything.

Because I knew that all this grief would come to pass, I had an action plan. I had not, however, planned for Dee's death. I believe now that this carried me as low as I had ever gone. I was truly in the depths of a depression—and I knew it.

On a Monday morning, after spending the weekend alone, I was standing in the kitchen making tea. Suddenly I felt fear lock up my body and my mind. The room spun, I couldn't move, my legs buckled and I fell to the floor. I called June; she came immediately, bundled me up and drove me to the emergency department of a neighbouring hospital, where we waited for the GP to arrive. When he did, he called for a psychiatrist; let's call him Doctor Smith. He was the antithesis of a good doctor. So I excused myself, had the GP prescribe some heavy anti-anxiety medication, and June took me to her place, where I rested.

The next day I was in a new psychiatrist's office courtesy of a friend who was also a doctor. I stayed in the new doctor's care for twenty-five years, until he retired. The deaths had blown apart all the hard work of a decade. I was back at square one, with so much to conquer again: managing identities (gender and sexuality); choosing clothes; keeping the truth of my angst from friends—frankly, lying until I almost thought what I said was true; wanting to quit working but knowing I couldn't for my own sake. The psychiatrist and I dealt with issue after issue for years.

He was an entertaining man who had worked with indigenous people in northern Canada, as well as with patients in mental institutions. Often he would just tell me stories during a session, and leave me to draw conclusions from them for my benefit.

He made me work for every inch of progress I made, particularly in the area of gender identity. However, I could no longer function in confusion again. Once and for all, I had to know that I could function as both male and female, and be acceptable to myself as a he/she. The realization that I was grappling with these same issues all over again made me understand that I would never be well until they were resolved. Always the questions, the dreams, the night sweats, the waking panic. This reality was unacceptable to me because it made me feel so abnormal.

Through the prodding of my psychiatrist, I found places where I could bury my angst in the hope that I could lead a fuller life. I knew I would never return to the heydays, but I could still have life and enjoy whatever my own efforts brought my way.

Ideally, in a psychiatric interchange, the hope is to resolve a problem. We both knew that was not possible.

But achieving reconciliation was probable. That's what we strived for. At every session, it was necessary to address these recurring times of gender confusion and despair; we'd go at it, again and again, until I could hide the feelings. It was like going to the gas station to fill up an empty tank. I needed information (I thrived on new research), reassurance, and a dose of resolve. But, in spite of all the effort, I was always in that frenzied state of confusion, and felt guilty that I wasn't "normal." I couldn't understand why my brain wouldn't accept that it was all right to be a confused gender. Trying to blame my father for my suffering didn't help either.

Once I asked if I would ever be well again. The doctor couched it cleverly by saying, "Maybe in twenty-five years or so." That, after all, was when he planned to retire, and I would go on to another psychiatrist.

Though my sessions with my psychiatrist had allowed me to return to some semblance of a functional life, I had grown restless at work. My president was ending his ten-year term. I decided I would end mine too. I had been offered a tempting position with the Aluminum Company of Canada (ALCAN). The project was a feasibility study for the building of an aluminum smelter in Manitoba. I was to handle the public relations for it. It was a tough job to sell it to both the public and the politicians, and I had a demanding boss. But, it was an exciting challenge. The job also had good benefits, lots of travel, and a very handsome salary. I took the position, even though it was temporary, because I had done the job I had set out to do at the university.

Big mistake! My mental health had deteriorated dramatically, and the job wasn't easy. I enjoyed the creation of ads and informational films, but I was out of my comfort zone.

The pace was deadly quick. Too many people to greet. I experienced it as an invasive cacophony of ear-shattering voices. I was in a frenzy and couldn't find any way to incorporate noise into my daily routine. I was doomed.

However, I finally discovered a strategy that I adopted from meditation. I stumbled onto it in a discussion with Jocelyn, a friend who taught me meditation technique: Breathe in deeply through your nostrils, slowly exhale through your mouth as much air as you took in, then recite a mantra. Any phrase would do. After exhaling, I would say, "I will be calm." Using this technique in short intervals during the day, I did, in fact, experience calm. I also lowered my heart rate and blood pressure.

Some time later, with Joey, I employed another technique, which began by thinking of my head as my entire being. Then, I'd ask her to cradle and stroke my head, softly and slowly, in a loving way. This took away tension; then I would take a shower and run the water cold, and then hot, to create enough steam for a mini-sauna. This technique worked wonders.

Of course, these techniques were temporary. I had to find a more suitable work environment, so, after three years at ALCAN, I took an offer to be vice-president of a local, internationally-recognized ad agency in Winnipeg. Another mistake, but it led to an opportunity that opened new avenues for years to come.

Before I took the new position, I had a scare. My cancer of 1975 appeared to have returned in 1984. I was very frightened. But, after investigation, it was decided that the tumour was really only scar tissue from the previous surgery. It would be necessary, however, to keep an eye on it. I was restless and didn't feel well. Because of my family history, I thought I should have a will and sent myself into a frenzy trying to figure out the details. Silly goose, I was. The prospective tumour soon disappeared and I remained cancer-free for another twenty years.

When I joined the agency, I met Dawn; she was beginning her career after getting her degree in communications out east. After a year at the agency, I quit one day over an issue of trust. Dawn left with me, as did Ed, a well-known creative artist, and we formed a public relations and advertising firm. We had a large contingent of clients that came with us. Soon we won other contracts as a result of winning awards for programs entered in trade shows. By travelling widely in Canada and the United States, Dawn and I secured a solid base of clients; then we started looking for clients based in London and the Lake District of England. I knew the Lake District well and was certain that our photo promotional tour would be well-received there. It worked. We grew as an agency well beyond our expectations.

Dawn was an attractive, smaller version of my mother, with the same jet-black curly hair and striking eyes. She was fifteen years younger, and I fell in love, much against my own good sense. I know she did, too. Before long, we were living and loving together. Except it turned out that she didn't like the loving part. That stopped, but she stayed on for thirteen years.

I had a 2400-square-foot condo, so there was room for each of us to have a work studio and a bedroom. She did the cooking; I did the laundry and paid the bills. We were able to do what some people find hard: We separated work from play, and lived our lives with maximum energy. I felt like I was a teenager, or that an aspect of the heydays had come to life again. Was that Dawn's influence? Or, was it that I had found new work to engage me completely? Likely both.

I tried to suspend reality—the reality of growing pains again. Identity, sexuality, and the problem of clothes stormed into a tidal wave that threatened to overwhelm me. I resisted as best I could but it wouldn't go away.

Another problem was also rising to the surface. Although Dawn was accepted by my friends, I felt uneasy about not spending time alone with them. On the other hand, I felt guilty about excluding Dawn because she had no social life beyond one boyfriend.

A major crisis arose when I learned that Dawn wanted to be with this man. I tried hard to keep her from him. The male in me made me extremely jealous. It was hard to control. Soon he and I were vying for her time. It was ugly. Finally, she left him. I had won the battle of the sexes, but at an enormous expense, financial and moral. I had tempted her with travels everywhere: overseas for theatre shows in London over a long weekend; trips to the Caribbean for Christmas; fun times in San Francisco; time in Palm Springs. Great gobs of money (bribes) flew out of my wallet. I shake now when I think of what I did. I managed by pushing bad thoughts about myself to the far corners of my brain.

I was a big disappointment to the one person I wanted to please—my surrogate mother, Margie, the mother of two of my best friends. She had been a mainstay throughout my life, particularly after my parents and Dee had died. She was wise, and told me that I was making poor choices. Still, I didn't listen. I was obsessed again.

In 1990, I got restless in my working life again and stepped down from my management position in the agency, leaving Dawn and Ed in charge. I pursued an idea Dawn and I had developed after my Aunt June had died of breast cancer. The idea was to create audio programs for cancer patients and their families.

The idea took off. Dawn and I travelled overseas and throughout the United States and Canada to interview cancer patients, their family members, and cancer care professionals, about 1500 people in total. We used the latest digital equipment, and then had the interviews transcribed to hard copy to edit. By a stroke of good luck, we met Ange, who was the clinical director of a patient-directed support organization in San Francisco. In Ange, who had a marvellously soft British voice, we found our ideal narrator.

And we spent time with members of a survivors' group, who later came to be known as the San Francisco Support Group. We used their first-hand accounts of dealing with cancer to create recordings that contained information that patients wouldn't normally find in books or learn from their doctors. We also had the good fortune of finding new colleagues in Sarah and Matt, who contributed much to the three programs we completed.

In a total frenzy, I threw money at this project—thousands upon thousands. And I accepted money from other people who were interested in making this project work. Unfortunately, politicking by those who should have known better soon turned the project sour, but not until it had been named one of the five best programs by the United States Cancer Institute. That's all I have by way of memories from this period: just an award and the terrible realization that I had started to bring harm to Dawn, which would put us on the road to a total breakdown.

Living on the edge for nearly ten years after leaving the

university, my life had turned into chaos. Perhaps that's why I never fully healed. I had no strength left to fight for my life. I had fallen apart. I was too ashamed to see my psychiatrist for several weeks. I hid and descended into hell. In the end, my psychiatrist said, "You fooled us all."

I am ashamed now for my transgressions. Where was my judgment? Or, was I just too sick to judge correctly? I couldn't even go to the caboose to see Ernie and Mr. McIntosh. They wouldn't have been able to help me anyway because I was too close to psychosis.

......

DR. EDYE: Joy lost her mother and the wished-for relationship with her, her grandmother, who gave Joy love and support, and her father, whom she despised though she treated him with respect and compassion. The losses triggered depression.

Through these years, Joy made some decisions that served to increase her stress. She moved from a high-paced job, where she largely felt comfortable, to a job with a frenetic pace. She became embroiled in a relationship that, by Joy's account, was mutually destructive. Though she was ultimately pleased with the cancer-support audiotapes, their creation occurred during a period of obsession and poor choices. Joy describes her problems as being significantly more complex than a single diagnosis of bipolar disorder. One of her most vexing problems was being caught off-guard by words ending in "ion." They sound like "shun" and conjure up images of being shunned. The words and images are overwhelming, making it difficult for her to think of anything else.

At times, Joy hears unintelligible background voices that

distracted her. She also hears a single intelligible voice, sometimes supportive, but other times giving what is called a "command hallucination." These voices would be considered outside the scope of bipolar disorder and reflect, in part, the extent of Joy's difficulties.

11 Memoirs of Madness

It's said bipolar disorder is a profound mental illness. I believe what is meant by the word "profound" is that the disorder dominates one's life like a blade ready to slit a day or night to shreds.

For three years (1994 to 1996) I was on a road to utter destruction. My psychiatrist said, "It was a serious time." That does not mean there weren't times of humour, but I really needed to dig deep for those.

I was remote. I lived at the lake because I couldn't watch Dawn in her frenzies of finding a man, nor could I sit idly by and see her destroy her best qualities—openness and vivaciousness. By pestering her night and day, this new man in her life created chaos and confusion for her, causing her to retreat into a shell. I could observe this. She was frantic to be finished with our work project—a series of cancer programs entitled *Voices in the Night*—and yet reluctant to leave me. I think she felt a sense of responsibility because I was clinging to her. Over the years, we had "grown up" together, played together and loved each other, unconditionally. Now all this was going to the scrap yard, and each of us was trying to sort a way through the twisted metal heap.

My salvation was my writing. I would sit hour after hour at my desk near the window, pulling out words from somewhere deep down, listening to a voice other than my own (or so I thought at the time) feeding me excellent prose. It was the beginning of a series of manic attacks that went on through the summer of 1994 and during all of 1995. I had this overdeveloped ability to compartmentalize what bothered me; I put the trouble in a box bound with an elastic band where it couldn't hurt me. It was my survival technique, but only a temporary one. The boxes, which were filled with various psychoses, were piling up. I entered a full-fledged period of manic writing. I edited a perfectly scripted audio program in six weeks. A wizard had been at work, not me.

What did I know about psychosis, hallucinations, delusions? I thought those were for the really sick people, the "funny farm" inhabitants. In hindsight, I realize that I should have sought help again from my psychiatrist, whom I was still avoiding; I needed his help to provide an explanation of what I was experiencing and how it could lead to a break from reality.

To understand psychosis properly, one has to understand the basic symptoms: hallucinations, delusions, and obsessive thinking.

I'll be brief. Psychosis, which can be brought about by stress, causes a person to loose contact with reality. Symptoms such as hallucinations and delusions result. Hallucinations are tricks of the mind, which may include hearing voices and commands. For example, the TV can "talk," telling the person to do strange things, or spirits can talk, or there can be strange visual and other auditory experiences. Often the person who suffers any or all of these symptoms will feel embarrassment when the episode is over, or worse yet, may harm either herself or others.

There can be paranoid beliefs that might lead to delusions. Delusions are strange beliefs that come from flawed thinking, and are dangerous in the sense that they are likely to produce paranoid conspiratorial beliefs.

Finally, obsessive thinking, which plays a very large role in my disorder, happens when the mind gloms onto a word or an image that cannot be dislodged by rational thinking. In my case, whatever I am obsessing about is generally weird, or a product of guilt, and although I know it's unrealistic, I can do nothing to rid myself of it, until usually ten to twelve days later it "flies" away, and another takes its place. It's not a pretty way to live because there is no control over thoughts. The job is to keep it on the back burner so life can go on.

All put together, these symptoms are a recipe for disaster—full-blown mania. I experienced hallucinations, delusions, and obsessive thought at various times for three years. How I ever survived is a mystery because I was utterly mad. But I managed to hide it from my psychiatrist and my friends, though I didn't even realize I was doing so. I had turned into a hermit. Another mistake. I know now that isolation is the springboard of my disorder.

Whatever I was doing or not doing at this point was not in my best interest, not by a long shot. I needed to know from my psychiatrist about the very worst symptoms of my disorder, but I never told him about them. Maybe, deep down in my soul, I was afraid a suggestion might be made that I leave Dawn. At the very least, I expect I was embarrassed about my erratic state. I had no one to trust, no one to talk to, no one to "talk me down," to explain I was irrational, to tell me I needed to see a doctor. If I had understood this much about my situation, I might have (perhaps) stopped the acceleration of my symptoms. As it was, though, I was avoiding my psychiatrist, and Dawn, if she knew, was ignoring my symptoms, although I doubt she understood what I was experiencing.

I'll give you some examples so you can understand the full scope of what transpired in my slow slide into madness.

I had a conspiracy theory which involved the people who dealt with the administration of money for the cancer program. Everyone was a dirty rat, in my mind at least. An investigation later proved that there was some basis for concern; however, my response at the time was out of proportion to events, and the wide net I cast fell on some who did not deserve blame.

I also heard voices. One night, my voice told me to get out of bed in the middle of the night, when Dawn was sleeping, and go to the living-room. Once there, it told me to go from chesterfield to chesterfield, repeating certain instructions.

One set of instructions had to do with the rather phallic-like part of a large plant. I was to cut it off—ouch—then I'd be fully female. I didn't. Another set of instructions had to do with a candelabra sitting on a high library bookcase. It played into the moonlight with different shadows depending where I sat in the first living-room. The candelabra was representative of evil, and I was to watch it closely until sunrise, when I would go back to bed and sleep for an hour or so.

This happened every night, until I felt broken.

On another occasion, I was in my loft office. I was designing a cover, cutting and pasting copy for a manual on breast cancer I had written under contract. I went to pick up a pair of gold scissors (my grandfather's, used for some special ribbon-cutting ceremony). In mid-air my voice said "Stop." I did. Then it said, "Plunge those into your heart; you are a bad apple." I stayed still, the fear bubbling up, then freezing me. I struggled with this loud voice inside my head, then put down the scissors, and went downstairs in terror. You'd think I would have called my psychiatrist, but I was aghast at what happened. It seemed to me that the smart thing to do was to go to bed and sleep off this very ugly event. I was smart enough to know I was having "events" and I needed to be careful of this voice.

You might wonder how I remember what my voice said to me. I never forgot anything learned or said from fear.

I have always retreated to my cottage at the lake when I am looking for peace. During this period, however, even my stays at the lake involved bouts of psychosis. I knew that I was alternating. Rapid cycling is the psychiatric term for moving between mania and depression. I was not only alone in my thoughts about missing Dawn, but I was isolated. No physical bodies around, only the sounds of the forest. Days were for writing, combinations of words of madness with words of brilliance, coming from somewhere. I retreated to the forest at night. I knew every tree stump and bump on the footpaths. Once my voice told me to stroke my nose and say, "This is very difficult for you. I love you. It will be over soon." My lips curled up as I laughed maniacally like a character in a horror film.

During the off-season, when no one was around at the lake, I had a series of hallucinations and delusions in rapid succession. My voice had me out of bed in the middle of the night to sit and stare at the yellow glow of one candle flickering. The candle hypnotized me, duplicating a process used to break soldiers in the war years. The voice had told me that I would be busy from nightfall to dawn. (I have compressed the incidents, but you will get the drift.) Then the voice told me to look at the birch-bark tree photograph on the wall. Instead, what I saw was a V-shaped background in which the moon was setting. It had religious overtones. Did I think I was a religious figure? I don't know, but to this day, I still have difficulties around religious artefacts, something I am told is not unusual. Many people who suffer delusions believe that God is speaking to them.

Still at my cottage, I witnessed a dance in the gardens of the spirits and the voices of the lost souls. All my relatives and friends who had died communed that night, becoming friends at last. I was overjoyed. Then I heard the voice tell me to wander the beach. I knew every rock on the beach. As kids, my friend Kit and I would jump these rocks in our bare feet, so I could go without a flashlight. Thankfully, instead, I blew out the candle and proceeded to my grandmother's cottage on the waterfront. After I reached my grandmother's place, the voice told me to go home and rest; it said that "there was much more to come…" When I got back to my wee cottage, it didn't feel like home any more. It felt brutal. The voice led me to the bathroom mirror, where I did not recognize the person, only the blue eyes, but they looked crazed.

The voice then said, "Get on your bed and look out the window." There stood a zebra and a rat. I mourned for the zebra—my beautiful mother. "He" was the rat, and I wanted to stomp on him.

I was now experiencing serious psychic driving: the voice was in complete control. I had been conditioned by it. I'd been stolen. I had no brain. I was told by my voice to stare at the white light of the lamp beside my desk for hour after hour. This seemed to prompt a trip outdoors to the fir trees of the forest nearby. There I lay my head on a branch and was told, "This is your reward for doing as I say. Now return to base zero"—the desk and the lamp.

It was close to dawn. The voice told me, "Go to the lake. There, by a rock—you know the one—you will find a wedding ring. It proves that someone you know drowned there."

I was dressed in shorts and a mid-length English hunting jacket for warmth since it was a cool June morning. I went stealthily on paths other than I normally would because the voice said, "You can't see anyone because something will happen if you have to talk."

I ended up in the water by the rock. I forgot to roll up the sleeves of my jacket, but no matter, who cares? There! I found the ring! I had been right. Someone had murdered someone. I took the ring, elated at my discovery. I ran up the bank, through the yard of an old neighbour and family friend. An early riser, she saw me. "What are you doing?" she asked. I said that I had found the ring that solved the murder. She disappeared inside.

I snuck home by another circuitous route. I took the ring out of my pocket. It was just the broken ring from a pop can!

"Oh, dear. Better go and confess to Jacquie," the voice

told me, referring to my godmother, who lived nearby. I went into her bedroom, stopping by the door. She was awake. She turned over when she heard me, startled to see me. I told her the story. She said nothing but was calm. I asked her if her sister, Peg, who lived with her, was a lesbian; she told me to go home and sleep and said she would come up later to check on me.

Meanwhile, the neighbour had called Jacquie. Jacquie had called Dawn in the city. They decided that I was "under suspicion" of having a mental break. But no one thought to call my psychiatrist.

I sat by the desk, in the white light, to think this through. How could I escape from being found out? I couldn't; I was terrified. But no one came for me.

All in one day, all these events, worked by the white light of the candle.

The next candle incident turned out to be one of the two worst psychotic episodes I experienced during those years. On a subsequent night, the voice told me to go through the house picking out objects (which it identified) and lay them on the deck in a row to be thrown out. After I had done so, it told me to "return to the desk light." I obeyed and out went family treasures—my mother's clock, my dad's wrist-watch, mother's plates, andirons, and coal bucket. I put the items into my car, deposited them in a garbage bin, and the next day they all went to the dump. What a sense of relief I had that day; no more things to care about, to carry around. I was free of them.

After this second candle incident, I went to the city, but I have no memory of how I got there or what happened thereafter. The only thing I do know is I that went to the City Park's duck pond one day with a sandwich and a drink.

There was a black swan among the white. Of course, that was my beautiful mother. She was so gracious, gliding through the pond. It made me sob.

July and August passed. I remember nothing.

However, come early September, Dawn began her frenzy with a new boyfriend, back and forth to Toronto on weekends. Her behaviour rubbed off on me. Our home was electric with negative energies.

Before Dawn's affair began, we had planned a fall trip out west to northern California to see friends and be in our favourite part of the world. We carried through with the plan and drove down the coastal highway. The trip rekindled our soft feelings for one another, so when we came to Netarts in Oregon, we decided to look for a vacation property. The prices for a matchbox piece of land were outrageous, but we took the leap and put down an offer. Business had been good. We were flush. I was stupid!

In late October, Dawn and I returned to Winnipeg. She resumed boyfriend hunting and attending psychic fairs. I seemed to be grounded and was sleeping better, thanks to a holistic sleeping potion (later I found out that it was "dangerous" when mixed with my other medications). I had been to visit my psychiatrist but he didn't pick up on anything negative, so I presumed I was fine. How wrong we both were. He said later that, as I mentioned, "I had fooled everyone." No glory in that. I should have told him about all the weirdness.

Soon it was Christmas 1994. Alice in Wonderland had nothing on me. I was The Mad Hatter.

……

DR. EDYE: Joy gives a haunting description of her psychosis. At the time, things seemed brilliantly clear to her but terribly alarming to those she let into this world. The voice gave her extensive commands and Joy obeyed almost all of them. Somewhere inside, she had an intermittent awareness that she was unwell, but hid it out of fear.

Her medications were ineffective, and as a way of attempting to help herself, Joy took holistic medicine. The discussion of holistic medicines is beyond the scope of this book. However, it is important to advise the reader that medications—holistic or pharmaceutical—have side effects that can interact with each other negatively. It is important to be open with a person's practitioner, whether holistic or medical, to help minimize harmful interactions.

12 *Demons in the Dungeon*

One of my demons, which I had thought was my greatest friend ever, became my greatest enemy and took me straight to hell. This chapter explains how I got there.

Writing this chapter is one of the most treacherous of the book. I am very scared. I need to pick and choose my words carefully so that I can live with them later because I hope never to write or speak of this experience again.

Dawn had been to a psychic fair where she had learned the "magic" of using a chain to guide important decisions of your life. (I know now that this is a commonplace technique used by psychics.) Once I learned about the chain from Dawn, I had to know more about it. It was magic. If you asked the chain a question, it swung in a circle to the right for yes; in a circle to the left for no. I could know everything!

I bought one made of beautiful glass with a gold rope in the north of Scotland, and loved it. So I personified it and called "him" "Allie." Naturally, I asked him questions about his life in the Highlands of Scotland. He was an ancestor named Alastair Little, who had a wife and two sons. He was born in the 1800s and had been a writer until he fell on hard times, after which he went to sea.

I spent days finding out about him. He was my secret friend. I came to love him in the months that followed. "He" occupied my life. For several weeks I did nothing, from morning to night, but ask him questions and get answers that satisfied all my needs and wants. He was in my pocket. I held him. All I needed was a smooth surface on which to let him swing his answers! Why did I not understand that this was a dangerous game? I just didn't. Reason had abandoned me.

After checking with Allie, I had cashed in some investments that I gave to Dawn, telling her that I was giving her the year 1995 as a gift so that she could "find herself." She wouldn't have to work or look after me in any way. Her one job would be to rebuild her life.

What she did, of course, was waste the year chasing men; but, I was no better. I wasted mine talking to Allie and moving further down the road to total madness.

(My voice, which is asserting itself now because writing this chapter is so stressful, says, "Can I get the words out now?" Let's press on ...)

Between the use of Allie and a sleeping potion "prescribed" by a holistic doctor, I recognized, finally, that I was beyond myself. But I also "knew" that I could fix myself. Hide Allie, somewhere. Promise, promise that I would not use him. And, stop the potion. Even if it meant withdrawal, which it did.

Had I cured myself? No. I did manage, however, to achieve a balance but it would prove to be temporary.

It was March 6, 1995, I know that. Dawn had made arrangements for us to take a trip to Toronto to meet with a bag man—a fundraiser for our project—or if you don't like that term, call him an "angel."

Taking directions from my voice, I neatly packed my suitcase. I got everything into one bag—unheard of for me. My voice got me through the flight with the "white reading light," a beam that appeared and followed me during the trip; it had the power to hypnotize me like the flame of the candle at the cottage. I tried to keep my head down so I couldn't see it.

We arrived at my usual hotel in Toronto. Room 939. Oh, my God! I asked for another room but one wasn't available.

I began to panic: "I'll be okay then. No I won't. But Dawn will be here. No, she won't. Yes, I can do this. No, I can't."

I have never been the same since that night in room 939. It tapped into "my numbers." Three is my parents' anniversary. Nine is my mother's birthday. Thirty-nine is the year of my birth. Nines are evil. Sixes and nines are male and female. I was ripe for an explosion of manic hallucinations, delusions, and psychosis.

What followed was an extreme bout of my illness, a descent into dissociation, where the ego splits, and you hit the trasher for a lifetime. As my psychiatrist said afterwards, "This is serious. This is forever."

I have only fragments of memories. Dawn wasn't in the room; she was probably at a meeting I couldn't attend. My voice told me to do weird exercises, which I did until I was exhausted. Then it said, "Tell Dawn to come to my room at 7:00 p.m. sharp. Tell her to get her own room. There's something unnerving about this room." When Dawn returned, I behaved like I was possessed. Scared the heebie-jeebies out of her, the doctor later told me; so she left.

Around midnight, it's alleged, I started parading through the ninth floor hallway in my full nakedness. I rapped on one door and told "them" to get out. My voice said if I didn't keep knocking at all the doors and get everyone into the hallway, an airplane would crash. So I did what I was told, until one person reported me, apparently performing a voodoo ritual. The hotel cops came to the floor, but I had closed my bedroom door, believing I was "safe."

With the cops out of my way, I sat down, and began to reason with myself. From somewhere very deep inside, I got the impression that I was having a heart attack, from the stress, strain, and mania built up over the year. So, completely naked, except for a winter coat, I went to the elevator; when the door opened, there was Dawn. We began to wrestle. I punched the elevator button for the basement and down we went. I pulled her curlers. She yanked the collar of my coat. In the basement, in the hotel's kitchen, I raced through, knocking down plates, with Dawn in tow and two hotel cops not far behind.

I somehow made it to the front door of the hotel. I slammed a glass door in a cop's face. A cab was waiting. I got in and yelled, "I am having a heart attack. Get me to Mount Sinai."

I was as nutty as a fruitcake. But I ended up where I needed to go—the emergency room of a major Toronto hospital. The race was over. An East Indian doctor interviewed me. I uttered a racial slur. The next thing I heard was an Egyptian female doctor saying, "Roll over, I am giving you Haldol. We will talk later." I was safe, for the moment.

Haldol is a drug with which I had experience. It's a major anti-psychotic. The doctor didn't give me enough, however, and I woke up, slightly dozy, but alert enough to ask that I be allowed to telephone my psychiatrist in Winnipeg. He said, "Stay still until tomorrow, then you can fly home. Be quiet tonight."

I have never reconciled myself with that traumatic period of my life in hospital, so I panicked. "I can't stay here," I told myself. I got my coat, and ran. Two cabs were nearby. I tried for cab one, but I heard his door lock. Same with cab two. I tried to flee but the cops were too fast and two big guys in white coats were with them. I surrendered. More Haldol. More sleep.

Magically, Dawn appeared. She had my clothes and took me back to the hotel, where I slept for hours. Later Dawn was gone; I suspected that my psychiatrist told her to leave because I could do her physical harm. In fact she had moved to a room close by.

Then the doctor phoned my room. He told me I was booked on a morning flight to Winnipeg and said, "Eat bananas, drink tea, drink water, eat a little; you have been on a two-day manic binge."

I wasn't done yet. (I would soon learn the very hard truth of his statement.)

I had too little medication in me. I forgot what extra medication my doctor had told me to take. As I awoke from the deep sleep, I went into high mania. Way too high. I went through a purification ritual, as he told me later.

I thought the mirror in Dawn's hotel room would have restorative powers. I had come to believe that a mirror was reality. It would smoke out my identity, my true self. Instead, on this night, it tore me further apart.

I told Dawn that it was safe to let me into her room because I'd taken the meds that my doctor had recommended. So she did.

I went over to the mirror and stared at my eyes. ("It's in the eyes," as I am fond of saying about people and their truths.) I thought my "treatment" would be more effective if I talked to each eye, so I gave each a name. The left eye I named "Joy," the right eye, "Suzie." What happened next was powerfully chilling. The eyes talked to one another, and the process became a life review fraught with episodes of my bad behaviours. If I didn't follow directions, the eyes told me, then we'd have to start way back at the beginning. "My life was dismal," the eyes said.

Several hours later, I realized Dawn had gone out with her Toronto friend and left me to deal with myself. I went back into 939, and I slipped in and out of dreams (or nightmares).

Come morning, my voice packed my suitcase, neatly. I sat downstairs waiting for Dawn, who had returned after I'd gone back to my room. While waiting for Dawn, I began speed-reading the newspaper, or so I thought. In fact, I was scanning the pages, letting words that had meaning only for me leap out of the page. I took a limo with Dawn to the airport, and watched the hypnotizing, white reading light all the way home.

Bed begat morning and I had Dawn drive me to the hospital to see the doctor. He provided more explanations than I wanted. But I think he wanted to do two things: scare me away from Allie forever; and, make me understand the seriousness of what had happened so that I would pick up the cues, should I ever feel another bout of psychosis coming on as a result of stress or a memory twig, or something zinging out of the past. His strategy worked. I saw him every day for two weeks. He prescribed a major anti-psychotic drug, which, he told me, had helped to clear the back wards of mental institutions when people were ill-equipped to be released into the community in the 1970s.

On that heavy medication, I went with Dawn to the symphony. Well, I can tell you, I have never heard music like it, or been so affected by a concert. I called my doctor (as he had asked) at intermission and told him of the thrilling music. He said, "That's the drug talking, or maybe you've finally figured out that with hardship comes beauty." He was right on both accounts. In those manic times, the sight of a beautiful piece of art or the sound of a beautiful piece of classical music would suffuse me with heightened emotions of joy and delight.

Days rolled into weeks. I sat on the chesterfield, and sometimes drooled with my head down to my chest. I tried to read but had no concentration. I was broken. I thought I would never recover.

I could not go to the caboose for two years. It was too hard to imagine anything, even something as healing as a journey there. I missed "the boys." I missed them so much.

My psychiatrist had me see another psychiatrist for a second opinion. I had gone from having bipolar disorder to bipolar with psychosis to schizoaffective disorder, but I also had dissociative disorder, which originates as an adaptive response to overwhelming trauma. The fact was, I would never be the same again.

I spent the spring, summer, and fall at the lake. It was quiet, but more importantly, so was I. I passed the days reading, writing in a journal (my notes eventually became this book), and visiting with a few friends. Dawn would come down occasionally, but she was always in a hurry to get away. She had met a new friend, and together they were in theatre class and had other common interests.

Wanting to spend more time with Dawn, however, I returned to the city. I believed at the time that my hallucinations were no longer a problem. However, my return to the city resulted in one final, major, extremely harrowing bout of psychosis. Although my psychiatrist had explained the development and process of mania escalating to psychosis, I didn't recognize it when it was happening again.

It occurred in a dungeon of sorts, a large locker facility in the basement of my condo building. In our condo building, each resident had one large cubicle, with a padlock, for suitcases, photographs, what have you. Mine had the number 306. That day, I decided it was necessary to visit my cubicle.

I'm not sure when this entered my mind. But Dawn was going out that night to singing practice. I needed to steal away. Good word, "steal." I stole her car keys. (Why? I think to keep her from seeing that man.) I went to the basement at about four o'clock in the afternoon, entered the locker room, and my voice told me to lock the door. Of course, I had the key to get out of the locker space, but my voice told me, on penalty of some sort of punishment, that I could not leave this area until I was told "all was safe."

The manic behaviour started immediately. I had to identify all the lockers whose numbers contained either a three, a six, or a nine. That meant searching a labyrinth of over eighty-four lockers; my voice called them "dungeon holes." I did as I had been instructed, and of course, there were "dungeons" with the offending numbers for every storey in the condo complex. I went row by row and performed a ritual of reverence in front of each. For what seemed like several hours (I was told not to look at my watch), I performed rituals on each sacred number: three, six, and especially nine, to which great homage was paid.

I can't talk about the rituals.

I was so frightened by the numbers. I thought, surely, my voice would let me leave the area, but, next, I had to flatten myself against a brick wall next to my locker. I performed a number of exercises, and after each, I took three steps—exactly—from the wall. The exercises were painful and awkward because I had to bend and kneel on cement. I staggered, trying to drive away the hellish din of overlapping voices.

Next, I stood before the opposite wall where there was a red light and a fire alarm. There for hours I had to repeat and repeat that I was a bad person because I had Rh negative blood type and had been transfused at birth; now I was to be re-transfused so I would be pure. (At the time of my birth, a baby born with Rh negative blood to a mother with Rh positive blood was usually given a blood transfusion to avoid the possibility that antibodies from the mother's blood may have passed through the placenta and might attack the baby's red blood cells, something that may result in the death of the baby. The importance of the Rh factor was only discovered in 1937, just before my birth.)

This ritual seemed to me to be out of the annals of the Nazi era, about which I had been reading in a book by Elie Wiesel. This was a terrible ritual and I dare not describe it here for fear that it would incite my obsessive-compulsive disorder and throw me into the same terror I had that night.

The rituals ended at midnight sharp. I was told to look at my watch, after which I could go back to my condo, but

I was ordered to conceal the evening's events from Dawn. "Pretend nothing has happened," my voice said. "Apologize for having her keys. You took them by accident." I did as I was told, and Dawn was so relieved to see me, the keys were never mentioned.

In the hope of grounding myself, I made a supreme effort to quell my voice, and went up to my loft, sat on the chesterfield, and wrote a letter to my psychiatrist of twenty-five years, explaining who I was, some things about my parents, the hell of the last two years ... and a plea for help. It was a very sad letter. He kept it, and in 1997, when my mental health had improved somewhat, he gave it back to me as a reminder that my life could have ended that night.

He put me on heavier anti-psychotic medication, and for a brief time, some anti-anxiety drugs too. I have never had another full-blown psychotic episode.

From time to time I have what I call "the schizzies." These are mini attacks, much less troublesome and dangerous than psychotic episodes, that result from witnessing a word, seeing an image, being sensitized to particular sequences of events. A minor attack might last for only a few seconds; a more serious one can last as long as ten days. I go to the deep part of depression when the latter occurs because I can't figure out why my brain can't accept that these images are "rubbish." But it can't, and the rational explanation doesn't override the emotional feeling of a repetitive "schizzie."

Schizzies can take the form of the voice chattering and making observations on virtually everything, or a "cocktail conversation" of voices behind the veil of hearing. It's deeply troubling to hear yourself think.

Even at my worst, I never seriously considered suicide.

Even when I was desperate, discombobulated, isolated, totally stoned on drugs, or broke and estranged from myself, still, somewhere, I had a flicker of hope.

And here's the secret: You absolutely can survive a terrible mania if you get help immediately, get the right drugs, and stay on them. Also, it's important to create a focus—writing in a journal, walking, playing cards. Try not to sit, brood, and review what has happened to you. Phone a friend, but don't say anything that would be embarrassing so that you can preserve your pride and privacy. There's no need to feed the stigma that accompanies mental health problems. Unless your friends are exceptional and understand mental illness, they will only want you when you're well.

(When my friends read what I have written in this book, I hope that their judgments will not be harsh; but if they are, I will go on with the few good friends who seem to understand intuitively that life has dealt me a tough hand, but not an insurmountable one.)

Another important thing to remember is that even when you slide into a depression, you can use all the elements I've mentioned to create a workable strategy. You are a masterful human being who is unique. You can be productive again, utterly worthwhile, and life-giving to yourself.

Talk to your loved ones. Tell them you will be productive again; you will master this disorder. Let them know you're working hard to make a better life for yourself and to contribute to your community. Ask them for understanding. None of this is your fault. Be easy on yourself. You are a precious person.

......

In the early days of my disorder, I looked everywhere for information. Later in the process, I became needy for people with whom I could talk and share information. Groups were difficult to find in the early years of my disorder. Eventually, however, I was brought together with a few people through a psychiatrist, and we formed a group. We were all women with similar education levels and interests, and a burning desire to bring some mastery to our illnesses. A band of four sisters. We had no leader but we invited experts to our sessions.

We longed to grow—in ourselves, in our careers and jobs. Foremost, we were hungry for tools that would help us to manage our illnesses and carry on with our lives. Did I tell members of my group every secret? No, but I told enough stories and experiences, and received enough back, to make these years of togetherness of tremendous value. We meet occasionally but on more of a social level. Soon, however, we will need to become an education group again. With bipolar disorder, age brings on increased symptoms and more frequent cycles, which will force us to find new ways of coping.

Over the years, I have participated in two professionally led groups. One was formed for a course of six sessions on grieving, the other to produce a survey that would assist other women dealing with schizophrenia. Both these groups fulfilled a hunger to be with people who had similar problems. And, always, I took home an idea or a kernel of information to help in the management of my disorder. I recommend the group process as a tool of great importance in achieving recovery.

Most of all, in the management and control of your disorder, find for yourself the best psychiatrist you can, one who will support you in a style you can accept.

Remember this: Each human being has a spirit that will rise to the challenge you give it. We are human. We can fail ourselves. Yet we can heal in a sanctuary of our own and live well. At the end of 1996, I expected that I might come out of the maze created in the three previous years. I had hope, and hope is the master of the future.

......

DR. EDYE: This chapter begins with Joy's decision to write about a time when she was very ill. Her experiences were so engulfing and sticky that more than ten years later, she still feels uneasy, and perhaps that she's taking a dangerous risk by lifting the lid.

Her gift of "Allie" is rapidly incorporated into some esoteric and faulty thinking. Magical thinking is the belief that a person's thoughts, actions, or words can produce a result that defies normal reason, as well as normal laws of cause and effect. Most of us partake in some aspect of magical thinking, often in the form of ritualistic behaviour; we wear our lucky socks or carry good-luck charms. Someone can become so engulfed by thoughts and beliefs that he or she can become delusional. At such moments in Joy's life, everything had special relevance and significance for her, such as the code words in the newspaper.

During her second psychotic episode, Joy quite sensibly omits some of the details to the reader. She has chosen to refuse to revisit the powerful and compelling beliefs she had then; she senses the risk to her health would be severe.

Joy is sensitive to certain coincidences, words, and images that sometime bring on "mini attacks." Joy's inability to dismiss these thoughts and reactions to innocent events is a reflection of the unshakeable hold they once had on her.

Nonetheless, writing openly, for the most part, about her experiences, Joy gives hope and suggestions for people suffering similar difficulties. I echo her belief that there is hope. With outside help as well as her own work, Joy has proven that one can become aware of danger signs and takes steps to prevent a relapse.

13 *Dear Josephine . . .*

My Clickety Clack train had hurtled down the track without a driver—namely me, the engineer—for two years. Now, in 1996, it was a time for healing and restructuring. Time to pick up a strategy for living again.

At the risk of sounding like "Poor Joy," I really had done this pick-me-up-and-start-living-again thing several times. Each time I wasn't sure where or how to start. One thing was for certain: it would take time. I wasn't getting any younger, and it would take more time to land on my feet.

I decided that I could just afford to take some time off and spend 1996 recovering with drugs and talk. By mid-year, I was more physically healthy; but, due to nagging injuries, I couldn't return to golf or tennis, which had been wonderful outlets for my anxiety. In fact, arthritis had set in, affecting those joints that were abused through a heavy athletic career, and I realized that I was going to need joint replacements.

Nonetheless, I reconnected with several close friends

and spent time visiting with their children and grandchildren. It was a year that passed by all too fast. I didn't have much to show in tangible accomplishments, but on the life satisfaction scale of one to ten, it was a ten-plus.

By the summer of 1996, I finally felt well enough to write this book, and here's how it began:

> I think people are afraid of three things: death, strangers, and having a sick mind. I want a mind on which an idea can perch, not one that can suddenly become a Jekyll or a Hyde. My final hell would be never reaching my full potential. So I must make this effort to express myself.
>
> It's June 20, and I am at Victoria Beach in my cottage in the woods, where I feel my roots and cradle my aches. Nearby there's a sandy beach and wide open lake, which, I've learned, can be very treacherous in a storm. It's my kind of day; the wind is up and whitecaps are rolling. My spirits soar. I feel that I can take a stab at beginning the book, the one that will say what I am, what I can do, and where I've been, and also convey my thoughts around my fears, missteps, and years of anguish. (You may be interested to know the following words sat in a file for nearly eight more years until I was ready again to risk looking deep within myself for words that said what I meant.)
>
> I went to the beach today to drink in the blue sky and its fluffy patches of cloud because I needed to be alone to make an important decision. I cannot simply ride the rails any more. It's time to act and tell Dawn that life is not working for us any more. How will I do that?

The garden is in. The cottage is ship-shape. I have the perfect environment in which to do my work; this book demands to be written. For years my good friend Elaine has chased me to do the writing. I've chosen the subjects, but I'm still not clear about the content. I want to tell the truth. I'm probably going to say things that even my psychiatrist doesn't know, even after caring for me these many years. It's not that I haven't wanted to tell him; it's that things get hot-wired through my brain or my dissociative self, and I forget. But the truth is a challenge; words can be harsh. There's no room for denial. A funny little pill cannot ease the pain of a bull's-eye word staring right back at you.

Yet the truth must be my guide because I want readers to really understand that being mentally ill does not mean that you are disabled, marginalized, pitiful, unproductive, or must be a welfare recipient. I also want fellow sufferers to know that they can lead productive lives. My mantra is, "Do not hide. Step up to the plate!"

I am not going to write a soft story. My life has been one helluva train ride, mostly without the engineer in his cab. Only hard, clear words will do.

Next year I am going to put in a water cistern at the cottage so I can stay around the year. I want to live here where the world makes sense to me…

By the fall, Dawn had become totally smitten with her new friend, Hartley (not his real name), and I wasn't pleased. However, for the most part, life had opened a crack, and moments of joy flooded in, enough to convince me that I had the energy for another train ride. I began to do things that pleased me, decided to like myself, and started writing again. These were satisfying and productive times, but they weren't trouble-free.

I was anguished at the thought that Dawn would soon be leaving and hated the way in which she was preparing for it: a few days with Hartley, and then a few days with me. I could do a lot of things, but I couldn't lose the "lonelies" her departure would mean for me.

On Thanksgiving weekend, Hartley showed up at the cottage and demanded that Dawn go away with him. I screamed and yelled and otherwise made an ass of myself. Dawn went but returned later the same day. We talked well into the night; she apologized for the grief she was bringing to me, but said, "I have to do this. I have to go with him."

It was crunch time; I needed some help. I went to see Elaine and Ross at their home on the outskirts of the city and stayed three days. Elaine and I talked and talked and agreed that it was time to let Dawn go.

I had hardly seen my new psychiatrist. (My "old" psychiatrist had retired in the summer, delaying his full retirement until I was in recovery.) I'm not sure I trusted the new psychiatrist, but he was all I had for the time being, and I needed his advice. "Yes," he said, "Boot her out." I created a plan.

In January of 1997 I had reconnected with Dear Josephine (a.k.a. Joey), a childhood friend whose parents had been part of my parents' cocktail circuit. She is five years older than I, but we were schoolmates and active in the same sports. In Grade 7 I had an enormous crush on her, mostly because she would always stop to say "hello."

Joey's second husband had died only a short time before,

leaving her financially pinched. To help her out, while giving myself a chance to escape from Dawn's disturbing behaviour in a quiet space where I could write, I offered to rent a room in her house; she accepted.

I gradually began to move little treasures over to my new little room. I think I knew that, in short measure, I would move in lock, stock, and barrel.

My arrangements with Joey allowed me to put my plan in motion. I prevailed upon Elaine to tell Dawn that she was no longer able to stay in the condo. However, Elaine suddenly became ill and was admitted to hospital; so she asked Joey to do the dirty work.

I was so sad. Hartley had said horrific things about me and done terrible things to me. I always said I'd sue the bastard for harassment, but I just wanted it all to be over and pull the cover over my head. I had one final go at him on the front lawn when Dawn left the condo for good. I had to be separated from him.

For weeks afterward, I sifted and sorted a condo in which I had lived for nearly twenty years. Friends helped. Joey's wolfhound, Maggie, was with me for protection every day. (I feared Hartley might come after me.) But no one could help me with my grief. I truly loved Dawn and wanted the best for her, but Hartley was far from the best. The breakup has affected me for nearly ten years, and I remain sad to think I cannot ever speak to Dawn again; she has cut herself off from me and apparently refers to our time together as "dark." In many ways, I guess it was.

On November 29, with my furniture and belongings in tow, I moved to Joey's house in the city. I was home. Dear Josephine. My Dear Joey.

......

DR. EDYE: This book stems from Joy's decision to speak up for herself and for others who may be less able to do it for themselves.

Though the reader may question why Joy continued the relationship with Dawn, no one would question its intensity. Intense ambivalence in a relationship is a powerful force that can make it difficult, as it was with Joy, to break free from it. She continues to grieve the relationship, sometimes more intensely, sometimes less so. But she did what she needed to do to preserve her health.

14 Hospital Nightmares

My early days with Josephine were full and fulfilling. My mental state was improved and I was consumed by "moving in" chores. Physically, however, I was in pain after an unsuccessful arthroscopic procedure on my left knee. When the pain became too much to bear, it was decided that something more drastic was needed: a knee replacement.

I was in hospital on the first night after having the replacement of my knee. I needed to sit up to relieve the excruciating pain of being stuck all night in one position. The bed sheets were twisted. I couldn't move. I felt trapped! I needed my Josephine! I rang for a nurse. A few minutes later a man wearing running shoes arrived with a commode. I had to go but told him that I wanted to pee alone; he turned and faced the wall. Afterward, he stood behind me and wiped me! Ugh! No privacy. None.

I was experiencing anxiety due to my hospital experience with ECT. I thought, "If I don't behave myself, someone will put me in this hospital's psych ward." More anxiety. I couldn't control it.

Before the surgery I had been in almost unbearable pain. I had told my orthopaedic doctor that Tylenol No. 3 (with codeine) would upset my stomach. So he had prescribed oxycocet—a combination of morphine and codeine. It provided only temporary relief. Next I went onto a stronger medication, a patch with morphine only. At that point, I seemed to be tolerating what had been given to me in combination with my bipolar drugs.

However, on this night, a mistake was made. A miscommunication between the surgeon and the anaesthetist led to the administration of a narcotic overdose.

I phoned Joey at 3:00 a.m. I was in a rage. She came to the hospital and calmed me down, and did the same for the staff. Soon it became clear that I was reacting to an overdose, not having a manic attack. The drugs were tapered off, which then allowed me to recover from the operation.

Fast-forward to the fall of 2002. When I had the pre-op interviews for my next surgery—left hip replacement—I carefully explained to the clinical nurse that I was narcotized after my knee surgery, and that I was forced to wear a morphine patch to deal with the pain. I also told both the nurse clinician and the anaesthetist that I didn't want the personal pain pump because it had contributed to the overdose; instead, I wanted an intravenous drip. I also informed the nurse that the overdose had put me into a rage that had disturbed the staff and forced me to undergo special psychiatric treatment. I insisted that staff become better educated on the protocol for people with bipolar disorder, and become better informed about my case in particular. She said, "Oh, yes, we'll make sure that doesn't happen again.

It's in my notes, which each staff member reads when you come onto the ward."

Joey stayed for two nights after the total replacement of my hip, principally because we had been conditioned to expect something going wrong. No level of trust, yet.

On the first night after the surgery, I was wild. I ripped at the IV line and yelled an obscenity at the nurse, who didn't understand what I was going through; the nurse yelled back. Joey was with me and discovered that I had been narcotized again. I was on the intravenous drip with the personal pump; furthermore, the dose of the morphine patch had been increased by fifty milligrams. Joey asked if the staff had been advised of my previous problem. The answer was "no." No one had read the chart. Twice that night, Joey had to signal Code Blue. I was turning blue and not responding.

The morning after, this episode was reported to the surgeon, who then assigned a hospital pharmacist to ensure that I got the proper medication for the rest of my stay. She put an end to my worries about another overdose. Nonetheless, I was angry with the staff's incompetence and reported the staff member who yelled at me.

Unbelievably, my bipolar drugs soon became an issue again. A night nurse who didn't believe that I could administer my drugs said that she would bring them to me, but that I wouldn't be allowed to see them. We had cross words. She yelled at me and accused me of being an uncooperative patient. I yelled back, "Get me your supervisor."

The night supervisor came and I reported the nurse; the supervisor was sympathetic and said that she knew something about manic depression. (Clearly, none of the nurses on the ward, including the supervisor, understood a thing about bipolar disorder, or that it is the same condition as manic depression.) The supervisor and I lay my drugs on the bed sheets so that I could see them and take them myself. I was satisfied, but suggested this was likely to become a recurring problem during my six-day stay. "No," she said, "I will put it in my report, as well as your comments about the nursing staff." She followed through. All drugs were handled properly for the rest of my stay and I never saw the offending nurse again.

After the issues around the meds were solved, I had to deal with nightmares at home. I dreamt that I was surrounded by mounds of drugs over which I couldn't see; and then that I couldn't get at my drugs, which made me go crazy with pain, mania, and restless leg syndrome.

One night I woke up Joey. I was having a manic episode. We called my psychiatrist and she had me taken off the pain patch, thinking it might have been the culprit. Within a few hours, I felt better and more alert. Good thing my psychiatrist also has a degree in pharmacology!

Joey stayed with me because I was so afraid of having more bad dreams; in particular, I feared that a voice would tell me to harm myself. My psychiatrist was consoling and managed to lower my anxiety.

Unhappily, after the hip replacement, another surgery followed in June 2004 in the form of a biopsy for lymphoma, which came back positive; so, I had yet another procedure to insert a port to deliver chemotherapy. These two surgeries went off with no hitch—overnight procedures, no narcotics.

But, my six months of chemotherapy produced horrible results—terrible dreams and depressive episodes. It turned out that one of the chemo drugs, prednisone, wasn't compatible with my medications for bipolar disorder. After each round of treatment during the first week, I went into hiding. Only Joey could visit or talk to me. Furthermore, I couldn't sleep, which, of course, made everything worse; even a sleeping pill made little difference. My only respite was desk work, mind-numbing things such as sorting files and photos, because I was dumbed down to the level of an ant. The retching from the chemo also created problems because sometimes I couldn't keep my bipolar drugs down. Finally, we persuaded the chemo doctor to prescribe an expensive anti-emetic to keep the food down and the nutrition up. "You can make it through," I kept telling myself. "If not, you'll die." Fortunately, I had a bright light to help me on chemo days. My friend Lillian came to each session with stories to tell and diversions to entertain. Bless her!

The chemo worked. The lymphoma went into remission. At the end of 2004, Joey and I went to Palm Springs for a celebration with our friends, Elaine and Ross.

I came home, believing that the year ahead would be kind to both Joey and me. She had been worried and was very tired from care-giving for four straight years. But it wasn't to be. I was soon diagnosed with lung cancer, and major surgery was scheduled in May 2005.

We tried to line up all our ducks to make sure that I wouldn't have any more narcotic episodes. We had to get all my information to the doctor, the nurse clinician, the anaesthetist, everybody, and also put notes in all the files. I also made provision that Joey could come into the recovery room if I got into trouble.

In pre-op, the surgical team ran into trouble putting in the epidural to deliver the anaesthetic and pain meds, but, finally they got the line in. The surgery was longer than expected, which meant that I had more anaesthetic than expected. I woke up in recovery in the middle of the night yelling, "Bloody Hell. This is hell." I called Joey and a friend who is an anaesthetist; they both came to be with me. When Joey arrived, she told me I had been badly narcotized and had to be re-medicated twice to resolve respiratory depression.

I was in agony. They couldn't deliver more pain medication, so they re-anaesthetized my right side, which is the side from which the lobe of the lung was taken. I stayed that way for the entire seven days of recovery. Pain management staff doctors were attentive, and when I needed more pain control, they responded immediately by increasing the dose of anaesthetic. No narcotics were used. It was dicey getting through the day and especially the night; I had to lie very still to avoid unbearable pain. When it came time to start moving about to re-establish the lung's fluids, I managed to push through the pain, with Joey's coaching.

One day when I was sitting in my chair, one of the pain doctors came by to tell me why I couldn't use narcotics (previously, no one had known). She said, "You are exquisitely sensitive to narcotics, and in the future, we will need to be careful with you." I wanted to shout it up and down the halls so the staff would know it was the narcotics and not the bipolar disorder "talking."

However, I still had to endure the usual harangue about my drugs; there was no real nursing care; no one who really understood; no one to talk to in the middle of the night when I was afraid of my reactions. They placed a curtain around me, which became a living nightmare. I felt like I was in a coffin with a white satin pillow. I saw shadows on the walls and was "on alert" for every sound twenty-four hours a day.

My saviour was Joey. She stayed near the hospital, and like the retired nurse that she is, helped me to recover. Each morning at six she'd peek her head around the white curtain with a big smile. She'd stay for two hours or so, wash me, give me a back and leg rub, change my sheets and my hospital gown, and then go back to her place to sleep and do her own things in the afternoon. At night she'd be back to settle me down. I couldn't have handled this hospital stay without her. She did the work of a full-time nurse, and then some.

During the night, sometimes I could doze, but I was awake most of the time from fear that I'd get a visit by the bogeyman from the psych ward.

I came home scared. Slowly, I lost the fear but the pain remained. Before falling asleep each night on the living room pull-out, I'd look out the skylights at the stars; this gave me a feeling of freedom that was healing, and I did heal.

I've written this chapter because I have important suggestions for those who are bipolar and must have a surgical procedure that involves recovery in a hospital.

Pre-surgery Preparation

1. I can't overemphasize that the most important piece of information to obtain is whether or not you're allergic to any medication, but particularly narcotics. If you are, *let everyone know in writing.*

2. If the person you've named to hold your healthcare

directive is not equipped to run interference for you at the hospital and with the staff, then find someone who can.

3. Prepare a document for your surgeon naming this person and itemizing what he or she has the right to do on your behalf.

4. Put your psychiatrist in touch with your surgeon to discuss your hospital care. Arrange for your psychiatrist to have the surgeon's permission to visit you in a professional capacity. Ask your psychiatrist to give the surgeon a letter stating that you're fully capable of managing your medications while in the hospital.

5. Make a list of the medications prescribed for your bipolar disorder, and other regular medications you take, for your surgeon, the nurse clinician, and the anaesthetist.

6. When you have your pre-op visit with your surgeon, ask what he or she knows about bipolar disorder, and offer to answer any questions he or she may have that are relevant to bipolar disorder, your surgery, and after-care. To greatly enhance your safety as a patient, you must demonstrate that you are well educated and have the upper hand on your management. Be emphatic with your surgeon that YOU are to be in control of administering your own drugs. As well, have the surgeon record in your chart a prescription for more anti-anxiety medication. I say "more" because if you're already taking meds for anxiety, you want the surgeon to be specific regarding what can be added to the mix.

7. Have your surgeon and nurse clinician indicate on the ward chart that anyone who wishes to make a change in your bipolar meds must first consult with your healthcare representative. If your representative isn't knowledgeable in

this regard, he or she can consult with your psychiatrist, who can then advise the prescribing physician on the ward.

8. Above all, remember, you *must* advocate for yourself.

Post-Surgery Care

1. You must specify in advance that at the beginning of every shift on the ward, the nursing supervisor who comes on duty must visit you. Ask the supervisor what level of knowledge the staff of that shift have about bipolar disorder, and whether the staff will read your chart. You need to state that you manage your drugs and that the staff member who brings your drugs should stay with you while you check the drugs to make sure that they are what you take. Count out and examine every pill. (I say this because I have had several occasions when a staff person was uneducated and gave me too much medication.) Also be sure to speak to your shift nurse, especially at night. Tell her that you have difficulty with night-time anxiety, confinement, whatever it is, and that should you feel unwell, you'll be asking for an anti-anxiety drug that has been prescribed by your surgeon. If you need more pain control at night, sort that out with the nurse too. As well, if you need a sleeping tablet, say so.

2. At night, the staff is often extremely busy and have limited time to visit you. Nonetheless, if you are anxious, request visits and tell the staff member (whether they're doctors, nurses, or only assistants) why you need them. Never miss an opportunity to educate. I was lucky to have an older night nurse, who poked her head in regularly to see that I was comfortable. One night, when I was in pain, she got extra medication for me; another time, I was very anxious and feeling the confinement, so she sat on the edge of the bed and rubbed my arm, and then brought an anti-

anxiety medication. On a third occasion, when I was in the wrong position, she fetched two ward LPNs (licensed practical nurses) to lift me up to a more comfortable position, while she literally held the site of the incision. These efforts to be tactile were the extra edge of comfort that I needed to go to sleep.

3. You can ask the night nursing supervisor if you can have the same nurse assigned to you each evening. This ensures continuity of treatment, and also allows the nurse to become more responsive to your needs. On occasion, I have had a night nurse sit on the edge of my bed and ask about bipolar disorder, as well as talk about her family, children, and the like; when something like that happens, you know then that you're not just "the bipolar in Room X."

4. If you're someone like me and noise is a big issue, and you're in a room with other patients, don't get a phone, but do get a TV and use the earplugs to block out the sounds of people visiting your roommates. You can also tell the desk that a roommate has too many visitors, and that this is disturbing you.

5. I found the chaplain a great source of well-being, in a non-religious sense. Usually he or she understands the need for silence and will listen to your troubles concerning a hospital stay. A recent survey reports that eighty-one percent of patients could use some help with spiritual growth through the experience of surgery and recovery. The survey also indicates that some thirty percent of patients in hospital have a mental disorder.

······

One of the first things I did after coming home was get a Medic Alert application from my pharmacist. I have a chain that says that I'm bipolar, and it also has a warning: "Do not administer narcotics—allergic." As well, I've placed the list of medications on file with Medic Alert. I recommend you do the same.

During my five hospitalizations, I wasn't able to go to the Clickety Clack train to see the "boys." The external noise, my internal restlessness and anxiety, and the haze of the drugs prevented it. I sorely missed them in what were times of great stress and need. To comfort myself, the best I could do was close my eyes and think of something beautiful, and hold that image for as long as I could.

I know nightmares are often associated with surgery and hospitals, but you can find ways to make the experience easier. The prime focus is to take your miseries away by asking for help in the ways I've described, day or night.

......

DR. EDYE: Each and every one of Joy's hospitalizations has been accompanied by flashbacks of ECT and the psychiatric ward. She has offered a number of useful suggestions for people with bipolar disorder. Communication is the cornerstone of achieving good care while in hospital. If you can't do it yourself, and a person who is medically ill may not be able to think or communicate clearly, it is important to have an advocate.

Joy is extremely sensitive to narcotics, particularly their potential to cause respiratory depression. On occasion, as a result of narcotics she has been mistakenly given, or because of the combination effects of different medications, Joy had rage reactions, which were misinterpreted by hospital staff as manic episodes.

Quick and assertive intervention by Joey was instrumental in effecting necessary changes in medication. It is not helpful, nor unfortunately rare, that ward staff know little about mental illness and therefore harbour prejudices about it. To prevent ignorance from compromising treatment, a family member or friend can act as an advocate, mediate situations, and educate hospital staff.

The treating psychiatrist can and should be used as a resource when necessary. He or she likely has previous experience assisting the person through a crisis and therefore has useful suggestions about strategies of treatment and the use of medications.

I agree with all Joy's recommendations except one. People quite capable of self-managing medication before surgery may find their thought processes impaired by the combination of physical illness, the stress of the surgical procedure, and the impact of anaesthetics. Thus they may no longer be able to make rational and informed choices about their regular medication. In that case, some form of intervention is needed by informed caregivers. So I disagree with Joy's recommendation that a bipolar patient should remain in charge of his or her medications. However, I agree with her recommendation to watch and count the medications administered by hospital staff.

I want to emphasize that if a psychiatric consultation is needed, the treating psychiatrist should visit the ward. If this isn't possible, then I recommend the hospital psychiatrist and the treating psychiatrist discuss the treatment plan.

Joy (left) and Joey

15 *It's a Family Thing*

This is a letter Joey gave me when we celebrated our tenth anniversary. It allows you to see my situation from Joey's perspective, which I hope leads to greater understanding of bipolar and schizoaffective disorders. At the same time, I hope the letter will give you a better idea of how wonderful our relationship has been and how much it has meant to both of us.

Dear McDermy,

My anniversary gift to you is this letter about our ten years together, during which we have grown older and slower, wiser and wider!

After being apart since childhood, I'll never forget our first reunion after forty years. What a lot of living we had done respectively in the interim. When we reconnected, I was still in acute pain, grieving the death of my second husband and my dear sister-in-law.

You were the first to truly understand my grief because of your own losses. You were caring and compassionate, and insightful about all my needs. The book you gave me, *How to Go on Living When Someone You Love Has Died*, made me realize that I wasn't going crazy.

You'll recall that after our luncheon we got together at my home where we had long chats, which meant I babbled and you listened. You helped me heal because you had known and worked with my charming rogue of a husband (whom in retrospect was an undiagnosed bipolar).

The bond of friendship was once again established. Little did either of us know how lasting that kinship, love and respect would be, or where this journey would take us.

Remember my first visit to your shoe-box cottage, "Deeside," one weekend early in the summer of 1997? The weather was perfect; we played in the waves, built sandcastles, walked and talked, and laughed among the dunes. I was free—full of living and loving, ready to embark on a new journey with you.

As we gradually finalized our living arrangements, I came to realize how damaging your relationship with Dawn had been. Then I went through your first psychotic break with you. I panicked; up until then you hadn't really talked about your bipolar status. But I was thankful that my training as a psychiatric nurse allowed me to come to your rescue and talk you back to safety and reality.

Only after this episode, when you truly talked about your mental state, your love/hate relationship with your parents, your closeness to your grandmother Dee, and to the surrogate parents who had helped to fill this childhood void, did I come to realize that you had been a "discarded" child.

As our relationship developed, I was happier, freer, and rejoiced in our female bond. And I loved seeing you happy and riding high. Remember that day when you had forgotten to take your medication? "No matter," you said; we were having too much fun. I remember meeting a colleague from the office, who also had a cottage at Victoria Beach, who commented that I looked like a different person. I was.

Later that season, I spent my holidays with you to see if we would be good enough friends to join forces under one roof and share expenses. I remember that the walls of your cottage were covered with your photography and your desk was near the corner window. ("Don't bother me when I'm in my office," you said. I respected that because you were focused on a book.)

When I put closure to my husband on the anniversary of his death in a ritual of throwing flowers out to sea on a windy, stormy day at the beach, it felt good. I remember walking toward you down the beach and saying, "Let's go on."

I came to appreciate that with the exception of a few people—your grandmother, your aunt, Elaine—nobody knew of your mental anguish and challenges. You presented yourself so well to the world and avoided the stigma others often attach to mental illness.

In late November, when we settled into a new life in my home after your traumatic split with Dawn and several psychotic breaks, life went on: you stuck to your writing and I stayed with my full-time job as a diabetes educator. During this time you had the odd rage, some depression, and occasionally hypomania. But you seemed to manage fairly well with medications and always bounced back. I remember cradling you like a baby, and learning to shrug off your anger by walking away. You didn't seem as stable as you had been; you were on a roller-coaster. Several times you were abusive, both physically and emotionally; then remorse, which is part of the progression of bipolar disorder. It was difficult to see that not only were you in mental turmoil, but that physical pain had come to taunt you from the progression of your arthritis.

When I retired in 2000 and we moved to the cottage permanently, the surgeries started. In two successive years, you had a knee and hip replacement on the left side, each one taking its toll on you physically. It was tough seeing you deal with problems relating to mobility and depression, but I welcomed the chance to care for you. I know that the hospital experiences of two surgeries brought back bad memories of other times in your life, and that matters got worse when the nursing staff didn't respond to your bipolar disorder need and the heightened anxiety a hospital confinement can bring.

As your frustration increased and your mood swings became more violent, I was so happy your retired psychiatrist found your angel in disguise, Dr. Edye.

When we all agreed that you needed a new mood stabilizer to attack the more serious effects of bipolar that you were experiencing, I know it was very difficult for you to accept a "dumbed down" personality, but truly the drug made an enormous difference, and you were happier, more stable, and much more the person I knew. Those big blue eyes sparkled with life; fun and laughter began again.

I must admit that I wondered how much longer I could endure living with your disorder, particularly after the night when you lost control and hit me. I was frightened for both of us. This was totally different than working an eight-hour shift on the psych ward, turning in the keys at the end of the day and walking away. Sometimes I would go to my private space in the Duckhouse—and cry—for you, for myself, and for what we had "lost," such as walking the dogs together, or moonlight walks by the water, or for the carefree life we had started as two "free" people.

By 2002 I had become your "family" in all ways, giving love, loyalty, PATIENCE, insight and education to support this woman of all seasons. I also found new respect for you as an individual. Your dedication to the management of the disorder, your courage in the face of growing symptoms with age, your determination to continue your creative flow, all this made me proud to be your family.

And still your secret was safe with me. Even my three children didn't know the extent of the turmoil we had been through together. I know there were many times when you worried that I'd had "enough." But I was committed to seeing you through whatever came our way.

Eventually, I came to understand your gender and

sexuality issues with help from your psychiatrist. I "knew" about these, without being told. They were a charming part of you, even though I knew they brought you great anguish when trying to fit into upper crust society. I'm so glad that I was able to assure you that we were in a different place and you could be you. It was the freedom that you needed and longed for all your life.

Then you walked out of the shower one day and said, "Our lives will never be the same now. I have a lump in my armpit." At that moment, we knew that normalcy had escaped us. Struggling through the excisional biopsy for lymphoma, then the insertion of a port for the course of high-dose chemotherapy, we went through days of agony. But the end of treatment came, and when we celebrated in Palm Springs with Elaine and Ross again, we thought we were coming home to an easier life.

The year 2005 began with both of us full of plans for the year. You were short on energy but we managed. Then, boom! A CT scan revealed the shadow on your right lung. We had so much despair over this cancer, particularly when only months later you had a shadow in the left lung. Watch and wait. Such a cloud over our heads.

I still marvel that you finished *A Stony Path: Guidance for Women with Gynecologic Cancers*.

After we'd survived a nasty five years, I was so happy when we finally got the good news that your cancers had gone into remission. But who would have thought that a third shoe was going to drop and I was going to need surgery for ureter and kidney pelvis cancer? And who would have thought we'd get more good news and that my cancers would turn out to be low-grade and non-invasive, and require no further treatment? In spite of our misfortunes, somehow we've also been blessed.

Thankfully, it's now 2006 and we've come home to our place of peace and healing in the boreal forest. We both hope we have had curative surgeries. Our focus is no longer on any other possibility. It's on life.

Although Maggie, the wolfhound, and Ginny have left us for Doggie Heaven, our feral cat, Luke, is happy in his corner of the world. We can make this a summer to enjoy, no matter what comes our way. Thank goodness we have friends who are near and dear.

Aside from giving you my take on some of the highs and lows we've been through, I also wanted to add a note about what we've learned:

1. The progression of bipolar disorder increases with age, which results in some loss of cognition; we've learned we can cope with that by having smaller intimate social gatherings.

2. We have learned the critical value of a knowledgeable and supportive psychiatrist, and that a family member needs to be involved with the doctor to be part of the support network and voice concerns.

3. Family members need to be supportive and insist on proper medication management.

4. Family members also need to develop skills to cope with "schizzies" and depression.

5. Family members must encourage and give purpose, focus, and vision to the life of the person with bipolar disorder. They should rejoice in that person's

accomplishments, encourage pursuits that are worthwhile, and limit invitations into "the circle of knowing" to friends whom the sufferer feels are safe and are loving.

6. Family and friends should establish boundaries for what they will and will not "tolerate" in the way of behaviours.

I have been a consoling mother, a sister confidant, resident house manager, chief cook, bottle washer, and the "Philadelphia Psychiatrist." You, Joy, have been our money manager, playmate (but, you're a poor loser at gin rummy and Scrabble!), grateful patron of Jo's Diner (daytime), and Josephine's Cuisine (fine dining in the evening).

We have great respect for the contributions we make to each other's life. With persistence and consistency, love and respect, we have made it through these years and come out strong, still laughing, crying, and fighting.

I must say that I didn't know what I was getting into at that first luncheon; perhaps it's just as well. I do know that I wouldn't have missed the intrigue of the train ride while witnessing the bravery you've shown in the face of crushing odds. You are a dear matey.

May our continued journey be a bit smoother as we celebrate each day.

Happy Anniversary! And thank you for the ride.

Your Victoria Josephine

P.S. Could we move into the slow lane now?

……

DR. EDYE: Joey participated in a few sessions when Joy was beginning treatment with me. As Joy's chosen family member, she was able to make observations and ask questions. She has also been welcome to attend sessions and telephone me whenever needed, and has done so.

Joey is the first person with whom Joy has risked full disclosure and this has been an enormously positive decision for Joy because Joey has treated Joy with respect and dignity. Their relationship demonstrates that a healthy relationship is needed to support each and every one of us. This is not to suggest, however, that there have not been many bumps along the way.

Joy may have been able to sequester her episodes of irritability had she lived alone. When it became evident that these episodes were becoming more frequent and had become physical on occasion, a decision was made to have a trial of a mood stabilizer. This medication has successfully treated Joy's irritability, though it has been less successful in helping her with the lows or depressions.

These two women are tremendously nurturing and supportive towards each other and have never lost their sense of humour.

16 The Roundhouse

Into the roundhouse comes Clickety Clack. My Bipolar Express is due for maintenance.

Mr. McIntosh and Ernie greet me as I step onto the platform in the morning's light. They have missed having me on part of the journey, yet clearly understand that I was absent at times during the journey because I was ill. This morning I am fit as a fiddle. I want to touch the train to know it's real, even though it's not.

The roundhouse is truly a gigantic dome, where each train finds an appropriate track for maintenance and retooling. For example, should a train need brake work, it would pull into lane one. As soon as its workings have been inspected and repaired, if necessary, it will be shunted to a spot where it can await the cars needed for its next run.

Like the train in the roundhouse today, I require a fresh car wash and checkup. Tomorrow I will go to my regular bi-weekly appointment with my psychiatrist, Frances, and tell her this train ride has revealed some faulty ties in the track. However, I am well. I might even be ready for another assignment.

The next day I tell Frances that, not long ago, I attended an open forum on schizoaffective and schizophrenia, where a patient and three psychiatrists presented new research information. During the Q & A, I asked a question about the progression of my disorder, given I was about to turn sixty-seven. The psychiatrist I liked the best, because he had a well-developed sense of humour, said to me by way of preamble: "First, let me congratulate you, because in our city you are one of the long-time survivors of this illness." Then, he went on to say that with aging I would have more episodes. And that the episodes will become worse and more frequent. There would be cognition difficulties, more symptoms, more cycling between hypomania or mania and depression, and a general need, usually, to bump up my medication or make changes to my regime.

This news gnawed at me for weeks. But, eventually, I came to accept that I would have to meet the challenge to the best of my ability. Knowing what is to come, I can say again that I'm happy I "front-end loaded" my life. I worked hard to see, experience, do, and enjoy the important things earlier in my life, so there would be no regrets later.

What is the "take-away" message of this book? By continually adding to my coping tools, I can say that my overall life satisfaction gets a score of seven out of ten. As in many stories, there isn't a completely happy ending. Nonetheless, I tackled life, dealt with the challenges and ups and downs, and did the best I could. I am a survivor.

When I was fifteen and my disorder began to emerge, I had the optimism of youth, believing that "tomorrow will be a better day." Remarkably, I never let that mantra go. As a result, I had a great career filled with accomplishments and professional awards, and also travelled extensively. Most of all, I was present. That's the ultimate goal. We should deal with our disorders head-on, not hide from them. We should "do in spite of"; that is our uniqueness. We should look at the beauty around us, find occasions to laugh, and remain loyal and loving to friends and family.

I am grateful that these old bones carried me through a great sporting career and gave me the ability to smash a tennis ball or smack a golf ball. Now, with systemic arthritis and the aftermath of lung cancer, I am less mobile and short of breath, though I can still walk.

I'm also grateful that I still take pleasure in the mission of my life, which is to write. Writing allows me to shore up my sense of self and feel that I'm making a contribution. However, while writing, I must guard my fragile identity and watch for signs of bipolar symptoms, particularly mania and psychosis. To protect myself, I try not to become overtired, sit alone for too long, or work for more than three hours at a stretch. I also need exercise and sensible nutrition. If I pay attention to all these things, I feel safe and life is smooth and grand, in the main.

On the flip side, in the last ten years I have found that I meet stressors again and again. It seems I'm hard-wired for manic behaviour more than I was in my forties and fifties, and cycling into depression is faster. Kay Redfield Jamison, whom I quoted earlier, talks in her book *The Unquiet Mind* about the excesses, dangers, and consequences of her own bipolar cycles. She says, "It's not like depression's an innocuous thing. You know, in addition, to being a miserable, awful, non-constructive state, for the most part, it also kills people. Not only suicide, but also higher heart disease, lowered immune response, and so on."

Sometimes I am paralyzed, completely unable to decide what set of tools to use to counter the behaviours. No medication handles all my symptoms. I stop at various stages now and ask myself, "What do you need?" Sometimes it's a friend, sometimes a walk with Joey, or some time on the beach. I battle symptoms every day now. I must learn to accommodate these culprits and their chronicity. My challenge is to let my symptoms worm their way into my consciousness and find a place of rest. I have to practise patience and remember that I have a reason to live my life to its current potential. I know my life has been diminished, but I can contribute. If I take this approach, doesn't it follow that I'm living a good life? Everyday I work at accepting that I do.

I believe that all of us, whatever our circumstances or challenges, must let go and accept that our full-time job is to come to terms with knowing that our lives may never resemble what we wanted or hoped for, but that needn't prevent us from living meaningfully. We're all in recovery from some act perpetrated by ourselves or others. However, by taking the time to know ourselves, we can push on with our lives and may even find a way to turn the tables on bad decisions.

While my train is being re-tooled in the roundhouse, I am aware that I have adopted a new style of living. I have chosen to let people see and know my inner machinery and all its defects. Many years ago, in my twenties and thirties, I wasn't capable of telling my friends my "dark secrets." I was afraid that I'd be stigmatized and that the news might get back to my employers. Even I didn't have all the information about my conditions then; how could my friends have understood?

Now it's time to be honest, but not because I want my friends to say, "Oh, no. I should have been there to help you." Rather, I simply want them to accept me as I am, something I need and want so badly in my senior years.

Remember the small boxes I told you about? I put my troubles and scared thoughts into them, placed rubber bands around them, and left them on the shelf of the caboose. Of course, this is imagery. It allows me to believe that one problem after another has been put to rest. I'm going through these boxes in my imagination, while also going through my real life boxes of photographs, papers, books. Everything I didn't want is going either to the dump or the fireplace. It feels good.

I am also repairing relationships that were damaged by mistakes in judgment. I want to heal myself and rebuild a connection to my lost friends. I've found that there are some wonderful surprises in this process.

I am also attending more to my sense of spirituality. Here I speak only for myself. I enjoy the sounds of the birds, the smells of the earth in spring, the surf of the lake, the sway of the trees in a windstorm, the soft falling of golden leaves, the freshly fallen snow on giant firs. I've found spiritual sustenance in all the seasons and the voluptuousness of life.

Even though I've had enormously disturbing incidents with religious artifacts, sometimes early on Sunday mornings I attend a little ecumenical church in the village. I sit in the wee church and watch the sun play on the stained glass windows, while Joey practises the piano, which she plays during the service; her playing is an important part of my spiritual awareness.

Before I finish this final chapter, there are three subjects I want to mention. First, I've learned in the course of writing the book that I may have been unkind in my references to my parents. I realize now that not only was I a surprise in their lives, I was an intrusion that strained a bond that was already weak. I want to believe that I brought some happiness into their lives in the form of accomplishments and grace—and I'll leave it at that.

I also want to leave a message for the psychiatrist who said I would be unable to continue my writing career: Never under-estimate the power of the human spirit. I did do what you said would never be possible. For forty years, the little train, Clickety Clack, stayed on the track, more or less. Every so often a trestle bridge went out and this disturbed the engine—the circuitry of my brain. In the main, however, if I concentrated and worked with my toolbox, I could go on into the night. I could keep the train on the tracks because I knew that the boys in the caboose believed in the engineer.

Finally, on the very day that I'm finishing this book, I've been struck by a powerful bout of obsessive-compulsive disorder (OCD). I wish that I could turn to someone who could make it all go away. I am dizzy; my blood pressure has soared, my knees and hands are shaking, and the pit of my stomach aches. There is no cure. What to do?

I think of my toolbox, but sometimes I can't because I get battle fatigue. I am out of gas today. I have to sit with these symptoms until I can attain an equilibrium. No amount of thinking will work it out; it will just send my mind into a perpetual merry-go-round. When I have the gumption, there is only one proven course. I focus on something real: I work at a desk or do physical work that has a clear goal, and nurture the hope that the feelings attached to OCD will diminish and that in time each recurring thought will lessen and finally disappear.

I don't have all the answers, only some experiences that seem to work, most of the time. The key is to use the right tools to cope, solve, and then move on with purpose. An affirmation also helps: "This is only a passage; I can live this day and have a rewarding life. There is a tomorrow coming. I can do it." Here are my life-sustaining suggestions:

1. Get a good psychiatrist.
2. Maintain your regimen of medications.
3. Be honest.
4. Be hopeful.
5. Listen to and trust yourself: there is value in your own voice.
6. Establish family sessions with your psychiatrist to track your well-being and share information.
7. Keep a clean house, that is, if you've harmed someone, you must take responsibility and make amends immediately. If you don't, you'll reap what you've sown.
8. Join a group; it can be your lasting pillar of strength.

Finally, a passage taken from Emily Dickinson:

Hope is the thing
with feathers
that perches in the soul
and sings the tune
without the words
and never stops at all.

......

DR. EDYE: Joy writes of the changes she has recently noticed in her cognitive abilities. With aging, difficulties associated with bipolar disorder tend to be more pronounced. Mood changes may become more frequent and more severe. As a result, medications that were previously helpful or in balance may need to be changed.

Above all, Joy works hard at being present in the moment. She can no longer maintain her previous levels of professional and physical activity. One of her challenges has been to find meaning in her life as it is now. Her goal is to be productive. She can't work for a long time, but she does what she can and then rests. Some days she is too fatigued or depressed to work. But she gets back on track when she can, and that is all any of us can do.

Joy continues to have challenges with both her physical and mental health. Throughout her many trials and tribulations, she has never given up hope or quit trying to do the best she can. This is her most important message.

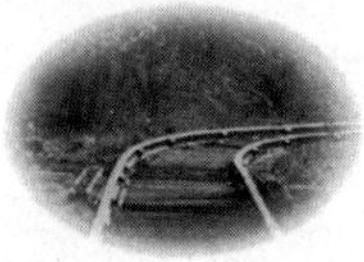

Epilogue

Endings, for me, are beginnings too.

At the end of *Clickety Clack*, I did, finally, say goodbye to the men in the caboose, those gentle friends of my imagination who coddled and soothed me for so many years. They were there because others were not. They helped clean my engine, so I could push on through my own mountain pass. I bless them for the journey. I will remember …

For many years, I couldn't look at myself in the mirror. That has come to an end too. I stare at myself in the mirror. Once I saw a stranger; now I see an old woman for whom life was punishing, but who looks forward to each new day with its fresh challenges and appealing opportunities.

My relationship with Dr. Edye, my psychiatrist, has had an ending and then a new beginning, too. Where once a single word from her was the only beacon of light available to me, we now speak in sentences. I am atop a mountain of feeling. I allow myself to feel, even to cry, in our sessions. I am sad, sometimes, for what might have been in my life;

at other times, I am grateful for the opportunities and successes that followed; and still, at other times, I look forward to the unknown.

I came to Dr. Edye through one door and have come out through another, equipped with a new sense of myself and a new awareness of self-respect. However, the journey is never over. On a good day, I can run my world; on a bad day, I can't count my toes. There's no science to it. A plan made the night before can be overturned tomorrow. This disease is a robber of plans. Ultimately, there can be no plan because making one sets you up for failure. The only plan is the moment.

I benefit greatly from other people's plans because they provide a structure that allows me to maintain some order in my own life. I can also gain a semblance of sanity from other people's voices; and sometimes the mere presence of others can keep me rooted in reality.

To this day I have feelings of a bomb inside, which unpleasant feelings and memories can cause to explode into chaos. Is it better to work it out? Or should I compartmentalize the fear and let other parts of my brain work on a project until calm arrives? Do I bury an issue and carry it forward to some other day when I'm stronger? These choices have to be made, and all of them are hard.

I've learned that the past has a great hold on the present, that the worst kind of pain is heartbreak, and that one craves the truth only when one can see a shimmer of hope. I've also learned to value the ordinary.

I have done my best to seek peace, and I hope that I've done no harm to anyone along the way. My wish for every reader is that you find a place of peace in your life, if even for a moment.

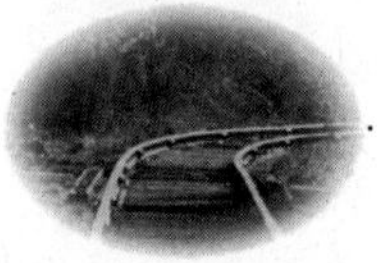

Index

Adamson, Josephine ("Joey"), 58, 59, 61, 74, 104, 112, 145, 146, 149–54, 158, 160–69, 173, 174
Aluminum Company of Canada, 111
Association of University Information Officers, 99
A&W, 86, 87, 89

bipolar disorder (*see also* manic depression; depression; mania)
  age of onset, xvi, xix
  associated illnesses, xvi, xix
  heritability of, xix
  management of in case of surgery, 154–9
  support of family, 167
  symptoms of, xvi, xviii, 103, 104, 118, 122, 167
  treatment of, xvii, 75, 105
Black, Mrs., 42, 43
Bradlee, Ben, 97
Brandon Mental Health Centre, 76

cancer patients, audio programs for, 115
Commonwealth Congress, 97, 101

Daphne (friend), 6, 22
Dawn, 58, 113–15, 118, 121, 122, 125, 126, 128–35, 137, 14–7, 162, 163
"Dee" (grandmother). *See* Little, Lou ("Dee").
depression, xviii, 10, 46–9, 51, 54, 57, 64, 65, 75, 79, 95, 109, 116, 122, 137, 138, 150, 151, 153, 167, 172. *See also* bipolar disorder;

manic depression.
Diane (childhood friend), 22
dissociative disorder, 134

Ed (work colleague), 113, 115
Edye, Frances W., xv, xvii, xix, 53, 54, 61, 178, 179
  medical commentary by, 11, 17, 34, 45, 61–3, 78, 79, 89, 100, 116, 117, 127, 140, 141, 147, 158, 159, 169, 177
Elaine (friend), 28, 59, 144–6, 152, 163, 166
Electroconvulsive therapy (ECT), 51, 64–84, 86

Floyd (gardener), 8, 9, 30
Freda (maid), 7–9

Gayle (childhood friend), 22
gender identity, 20, 23–6, 29, 34, 48–53, 55, 59–62, 81–3, 89, 110, 111
Government House (Manitoba), 37–9, 41–4, 46, 47, 96
Great Flood (Manitoba, 1950), 23

Haldol, 131, 132
Hartley, 144–6
Haruko (nanny), 13, 15
hypomania, 65, 92, 171

Jacquie (godmother), 124, 125
Jamison, Kay Redfield, 105, 172
Janie (childhood friend), 21, 22
Jocelyn (friend), 112
Johnson, Sara, 76

Kushner, Harold, 105, 106

Little, Glad. See McDiarmid, Glad (née Little)
Little, Harry, 10, 26, 93
Little, June, xxi, 2, 7, 10, 11, 51, 65, 107–9, 124, 143, 151
Little, Wib, 2, 5–7, 13, 26
Little, Lou ("Dee"), 1–11, 13, 26–31, 51, 93, 94, 102, 108, 109, 114, 163

magical thinking, 17, 140
mania, xviii, 65, 75, 95, 103–5, 120, 122, 131, 132, 135, 138, 151, 171, 172
manic depression, xviii, 10, 47, 51, 54, 64, 65, 105, 150, 151. *See also* bipolar disorder; mania; depression.
Manitoba Sugar Company, 5, 25
Margie, 114
Marguerite, Aunt, 24
Massey, Vincent, 39
Matt (work colleague), 115
McDiarmid, Gertrude, 38, 39, 41, 46
McDiarmid, Glad (née Little), 1–5, 7, 10, 26, 30, 31, 39, 40, 91, 95, 101, 102
McDiarmid, John Stewart, 36, 38, 40

McDiarmid, John Stewart, Jr. (Jack), 4, 5, 24, 25, 40, 47, 65, 66, 95, 101, 106–8
Medic Alert, 158

obsessive-compulsive disorder, xviii, 34, 103, 120, 136, 175

Parnate, 48
Patrick (childhood friend), 25, 28
Prince Philip, 38, 40
Princess Mary, 39
psychosis, 119, 120

Queen Elizabeth II, 38, 40
Quinn, Mrs. (babysitter), 9, 13

Ringrose, Madame (seamstress), 41
Rodgers, Don, 53

San Francisco Support Group, 115
Sarah (work colleague), 115
schizoaffective disorder, xvii, 103, 134
schizophrenia, xi, xvi, xvii, xix, 139, 171
sexual identity, 51, 54–62, 64, 78. *See also* gender identity
Sharp, Mitchell, 93, 94
A Stony Path: Guidance for Women with Gynecologic Cancers, 166
Strathcona Curling Club, 5

United States Cancer Institute, 115
University of Manitoba, xv, 6, 47
University of Winnipeg, 88, 96–8

Victoria Beach (Manitoba), xxi, 2, 33, 72, 143, 163

War Time Price and Trades Board, 5
Wiesenthal, Simon, 97
Winnipeg Ballet Company, 39
Winnipeg Grain Exchange, 5, 6

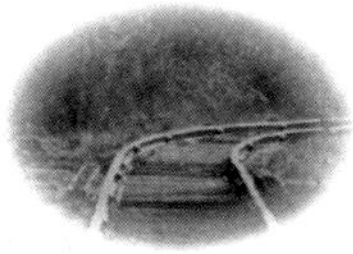

Credits

Always in my mind, in the writing of this book, was my grandmother busily steering the content. She is beloved for giving me a life.

Daphne Ethans, Elaine King, Janie Regier, and Jocelyn Samson reached out intuitively to support me when I lived in dark shadows, even though they didn't know my whole story. I am immensely thankful for their unconditional friendship.

Farther afield, I must thank Jane and Roger Gateson, Cynthia Powell, and Cyndy Hubler, devoted and generous friends who read manuscripts and offered suggestions.

I must also recognize Judy Clarke, a therapist and journalist, who pulled many portions of the manuscript from deep within me. She has supported this project with respect and understanding.

I am deeply grateful to two persons who were determined to help me give the reader a precise accounting of my life: my psychiatrist of nearly twenty-five years, Dr. Donald D.

Rodgers, and Dr. Frances Edye, my current psychiatrist. Dr. Edye's commentary has added immeasurably to the book's educational power; she also stood by, ready to catch the fallout from hard and hurtful times I had to revisit to write the book.

Dawn Holman, my partner in work and play for thirteen years, had a major influence on my life. During our years together, she was a thoughtful, kind, and forceful soul in circumstances she did not understand. Though we are strangers now, I thank her for the good years.

This book reflects editing assistance of Michael Alexander, whose insight, keen imagination, patient understanding, and humanity have been a blessing.

Dale Carvery, my ever-present secretary, offered friendship, as well as her skill in the preparation of several drafts of the manuscript.

My lawyer, Rob Giesbrecht, provided points of clarity and affirmation.

With respect and admiration, I acknowledge Kitson Vincent who gave generously to support me and the various steps leading to the production of this book.

A book must have a trainmaster. I had two: my publisher, Patrick Boyer, president of Blue Butterfly Book Publishing Inc., who had confidence that *Clickety Clack* belonged on his roster; and Dominic Farrell, who brought his talents as an extractor of rock-bed information, his calm, his management of the written word, and his genius in polishing those words to this project. He is a gold-brick man. Before my manuscript could be turned into the printed and bound book you are holding, Gary Long rendered fine service in layout, design, typesetting, indexing, and many other behind-the-scenes production chores. I thank Gary for his artistic attention to detail and am grateful that his talent and professionalism are part of the Blue Butterfly Books team.

Finally, the book bears the distinct imprint of my partner, my "Philadelphia psychiatrist" and in-house editor, my loving "everything," Josephine Adamson, who day after day listened, cried with me, and offered constant safe harbour. My bridge to life and my link to reality, she is a treasure.

JOY S. McDIARMID trained as a research writer. She held a number of posts in libraries, university, and private enterprise in Canada, the United States, and overseas during her thirty-year career in public relations and communications.

In 1990, Joy retired from her consultant practice and devoted herself to *Voices in the Night*, a series of audiocassette programs for cancer patients and family members. She co-authored three programs, including the six-part award-winning Breast Cancer cassettes.

In September 2001 she moved permanently to Victoria Beach, Manitoba, a vacation community on the eastern shores of Lake Winnipeg where she has spent each summer for sixty-eight years. She completed work on *A Stony Path: Guidance for Women with Gynecologic Cancers*, which was published in Canada in 2006 simultaneously with its release on the web for patients beyond the borders of this country.

In the past ten years, Joy and her companion, Josephine (Joey) Adamson, who is also her caregiver, have both endured treatments for cancers, all of which are in remission.

Joy and Joey enjoy their large gardens. They also take an active part in the community life of the village, which swells to a resort population of some 10,000 in a Victorian setting during summertime.

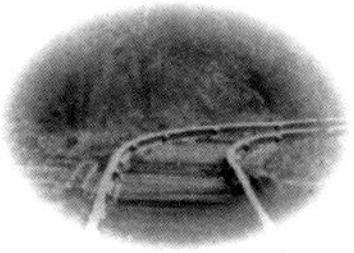

Interview with the Author

Traditional labels to describe sexual identity and gender were certainly not right for you, but in all areas of your life aren't you someone who does not fit or who does not like being put into categories?

JOY S. McDIARMID: Yes, you're nearly right. To fit, for anyone, is to be stale, perhaps even boring. As human beings we need challenge to prepare us for growth. That achieved, each of us is closer to our potential. At age seventy I am now more satisfied with my progress in areas where I have been tested.

In your imaginary "journeys" on the Clickety Clack Express, did you ever envision a safe and secure destination?

McDIARMID: Security is not a human condition. My train journeys were actually adventures, as well as being a search for human warmth and acceptance "in my corner of the world." To me the "destination" is not a place but a state of satisfaction.

In the book you describe becoming an enthusiastic photographer. However, while photos of you appear with early chapters, they are absent from later chapters. Why?

McDIARMID: When you leaf through a photo album, what do you usually find? People. Smiles. Life at a given instant. The content is unknown to you, unless the photographer sits beside you, giving explanations. What's missing is reality and context.

When I was a child, I asked my mother for photo albums. What I got was the cardboard frames of her wedding. No albums at all. I deduced their life was lacking in activity and people.

When I was older I wanted to be a photographer who travelled in search of people of all lands. I also decided that the albums of photos I had of younger years—the tough years—did not tell a story of consequence. At the very least they told stories of an unhappy child, in turmoil, engaged in "have-to" activities. Many of those photographs taunted me back into spaces of my mind where I did not want to go.

In any photo I took I wanted to see truth. I wanted to feel what I saw through the lens. I have a few photographs by which I can remember certain times, but true to my way of life, I have a "clean house." The photos of yesteryear have been burned, literally. I unleashed the turmoil of yesterdays.

What qualities do you believe are needed by readers who identify with pain and suffering like you've endured in your own life?

McDIARMID: Courage. Belief in self. Willingness to open up, to lay your story flat out so that honest help becomes available.

What did writing these memoirs teaches you about your life?

McDIARMID: I didn't set out to write my memoirs. I began this book as a story of a lost child and how that child weathered storms beyond her ability to influence them. That said, I did learn from the writing of the book. Teachings to take away from the experience include this major thought: you are what you are. Live with this productively.

About this Book

Clickety Clack is Joy McDiarmid's behind-the-scenes self-portrait about bipolar mental illness and one of the most ambiguous sexual identities imaginable. Amidst gender and sexuality confusion, this Winnipeg woman began to look for romantic love and sexual fulfilment: sometimes wanting to dress as a man, sometimes as a woman, sometimes attracted to men, sometimes to women.

In candid accounts of this paralysing complexity, which Joy tried valiantly to understand and express despite oppressive social stigmas and parental strictures, her insights about human sexuality and "living the lie" are startling even in this age of open commentary about sex.

This book weaves together her experiences along primitive frontiers of treatment for bipolar disorders and dramas of shock therapy in psychiatric wards, where entire years of Joy's life would slip by even as earlier years were being erased from her memory, with triumphant accomplishments in her competitive and stimulating world of advertising, university work, private enterprise, photography, travel, touring in her MG sports car, and skilful tennis.

Such juxtaposed experiences of defiant courage, supplemented with medical commentary by Joy's psychiatrist Dr. Frances Edye, make *Clickety Clack* a rare roadmap to life.